THE HOLY ANGELS

BY

THE REVEREND R. O'KENNEDY

(OF THE DIOCESE OF LIMERICK).

CONTENTS.

Part I.

Part II.— Excellence of the Angels.

Contents.

PART III.—FALL OF THE ANGELS.

PART IV.—PUNISHMENT.

Contents.

Contents.

Contents.

THE ANGELS.

1. THE meaning of the word Angel is messenger. That name is given to those pure spirits because such is the relation they bear to God and us. Their principal duty, however, is the same as the office of the blessed in heaven —to see, love, bless, and enjoy God for ever and ever.

Among the ancients there were many who believed there was nothing in the world but what could be seen or perceived by the senses. The Sadducees, for instance, did not believe in the existence of spirits.

It is the boast of modern atheists and rationalists that there is nothing but "Nature" and "the forces of Nature"; with them there are no angels.

Some of the Greek philosophers held that there were angels, but that these angels had bodies; not, indeed, corporeal, dense bodies like ours, but bodies suitable to their nature—thin, airy, star-like bodies. Some, even, of the Fathers, on account of the angels being represented as having the appearance of men, seemed to favour the theory of their having bodies. Petavius says that Irenæus, Tertullian, Origen, and others held this doctrine.

Now, Catholics say that the angels are pure spirits because, wherever in the Scripture they are introduced they

I

are simply called by the name of spirit. "Are they not all ministering spirits?" (*Heb.* i. 14). "Who makest Thy angels spirits" (*Ps.* ciii.).

The Fourth Council of Lateran has defined that "God created together, at the beginning of time, out of nothing, both classes of creatures, spiritual and corporal—the angelic, to wit, and the material; and then the human, as a composite of both spirit and body".

Even Aristotle says: "All nations believe that there are individual intelligences beyond the skies—that these are subject to no change and to no passion; that they are in enjoyment of the fullest and most perfect life, which consists not so much in action as in contemplation; that they have a king, that they differ from men, and are inconceivably more excellent".

2. *Question.*—How did these men conceive the idea of an angel?

Answer.—We can only answer by conjecture. Perhaps from the responses of idols or their prophecies; perhaps from the motions of the heavenly bodies, or from some extraordinary facts which were not to be explained by any knowledge they had of Nature; or, better, and more likely, from the ancient tradition of the patriarchs.

Cardinal Newman's notion of the angels before he became a Catholic will prove interesting : " It was, I suppose, to the Alexandrian school and to the early Church that I owe in particular what I definitely held about the angels. I viewed them not only as the ministers employed by the Creator in the Jewish and Christian dispensations, as we find on the face of Scripture, but as carrying on, as the Scripture also implies, the economy of the visible world. *I considered them as the real causes of motion, life, and light,* and of those elementary principles of the physical universe, which, when offered in their developments to our senses, suggest to us the notion of cause and effect, and of what are called the laws of Nature. This doctrine I have drawn out in my sermon for Michaelmas Day, written in 1831. I say of the angels : Every breath of air, and ray of light and heat, *every beautiful prospect is,* as it were, *the skirts of their garments, the waving of the robes* of those whose faces see God."— *Apologia.* (The italics are not Dr. Newman's.)

Now, what would our reason tell us ? This : we are per suaded of the innate nobility of spirit—but as it exists in us it is united with a strange and (to it) repugnant nature, hampering, fettering, clouding, perplexing it. Then, we say, if there be a just God, putting everything in due order— order being heaven's first law—there ought to be a world of spirit alone. Again, we look at ourselves and find that we are a compound of material and immaterial ; the material we find existing outside us, by itself, alone ; we look, there- fore, for the immaterial existing by itself alone, in this order —(1) material, (2) material and immaterial united, (3) imma- terial. If we look to the visible world we find this gradation : mineral world (in the lowest grade), vegetable world (nobler), animal world (noblest).

"God, who is a pure Spirit," says the great Bossuet, " wished to create spirits like Himself pure and immaterial —like Him, living by intelligence and love—spirits that would know Him and love Him, as He knows Himself and loves Himself; and who, like Him, would be happy in simply knowing and loving the first great Being (and He is Himself happy in knowing Himself and loving Himself); and for that very reason they bear on their nature a divine character, which makes them after His image and likeness."

3. *Question.*—By whom were immaterial substances created? or, is it possible to create them?

Answer.—It was God made the angels. Says Bossuet: "O God, who can doubt that You could create spirits without a body? Or, is there need of a body that one might understand, love, and be happy? You, who are Yourself so pure a Spirit—are You not incorporeal and immaterial? Are not intelligence and love spiritual and immaterial operations which can be exercised without the need of a body? Who doubts, then, that You could create intelligences of this kind? And You Yourself have not left us in doubt, but have revealed it to us."

4. *Question.*—But at what point of time were the angels created?

Answer.—(1) It is a matter on which all theologians are agreed, that the nine choirs of angels were created at one and the same time.

(2) That they were not created *after* the creation of earthly bodies.

(3) Some of the ancient Fathers, following the opinion of the great and learned Origen, have held that the angels existed for a long space of time, or at least for some time, prior to the point of time indicated by the Book of Genesis,

where (in its opening verse) it says : " In the beginning
God created heaven and earth ". Among the Eastern
Fathers holding this opinion were such holy and venerable
names as St. Basil, St. Gregory Nazianzen, St. Chrysostom,
St. Damascene ; and among the Latin Fathers, St. Hilary,
St. Ambrose, St. Jerome, &c.

(4) That is no longer held. On the contrary, the common
opinion—which it would be rash to deny—teaches that the
angels were created *at the same time* with the corporeal
world. The Scripture (*Eccl.* xviii. 1) says : " He who liveth
for ever made all things *together*". St. Augustine infers
from this that God created all the things of the world in one
moment ; nevertheless, it seems the more acceptable opinion
that the word "together" means about the same period,
without any notable interval of time elapsing ; and is, perhaps, to be understood of collection or community rather
than of time. The phrase "in the beginning" seems to be
taken here, as also in the first chapter of St. John's Gospel
(see Maldonatus), as meaning "in the commencement when
created things began to be ". Now, since angels are created
things, they seem to be included in this description of the
inspired writer. It is thus that Epiphanius, Theodorotus,
Ven. Bede, St. Thomas, Suarez, and almost all modern
writers, write and teach. The definition of the Fourth
Council (Lateran) has been already given. It says : " God
created *together*, at the beginning of time, out of nothing,
both classes of creatures, spiritual and corporal—the angelic,
to wit, and the worldly ; and *then* the human, as a composite
of both spirit and body ". The Vatican Council has repeated
these same words, and embodied them anew in a definition.

Now, the juxtaposition of the words *together* and *then* seems to point out the angelic and the corporeal worlds were created at one and the same time, but that it was some time afterwards when the human came into existence.

St. Thomas argues: The angels are a part of the universal creation, and form a regular grade in that creation. Now, no part can be perfect separated from its belongings, and God's works are said to be all perfect. But, the angelic world would have stood by itself, separated from the rest of creation, if it had been created before the sensible world; and therefore, to the eye of the metaphysician, would have been much less perfect than if formed conjointly and simultaneously with the corporeal world.

It is, therefore, all but a matter of faith that angels were created at the same time, *i.e.*, simultaneously, with the pre-Adamite world, out of whose "chaos and void" God drew the beauty and order of ours.

Obj.—But why did not Moses mention the angels in Genesis, when he was relating the works of the Creation? Why did he not give them first place, as they were the most excellent of God's works?

(1) St. Jerome says: Moses omitted them because he was treating of the visible world only.

(2) St. Cyril says: Because all he proposed to write about was what had reference to man.

(3) St. Augustine says: That the angels are meant in the word *heaven*, and even in the word *light*. If this were not well understood among the Hebrews, that people would come to believe that the angels were never created, and therefore eternal.

(4) St. Thomas thus explains the secrecy of the great Law-giver on the matter: "That if it were openly told to a rude and uncultured people, as the Hebrews were, and so especially prone to idolatry, that beings of such an exalted and beautiful nature existed, possessing such an influence in the world's providence and economy, they would, without doubt, have raised altars and sacrificed to them". Even Moses' own dead body had by God's providence to be kept secret from them.

It is true that in many places in the Pentateuch Moses speaks of angels, but in such a manner as above all to declare that there is but one God, and to testify that these are no more than His ministers, servants, messengers—and with such care that nowhere do we find it related that the Jews raised idols to them.

"God created the angels and the stars. How ancient the angels are we do not know; though we know that *spiritual and material natures were created at the same moment.* In all ways the angels are wonderful to think of, because they are so strong, so wise, so various, so beautiful, so innumerable."—F. Faber, *Precious Blood*, p. 9.

5. *Question.*—What is the number of the angels?

Answer.—It cannot be given. Nothing is known exactly of their number; it is beyond human calculation, like the stars at night. The number is indefinitely great, and all but infinite. The Holy Scriptures pretend but to give a vague idea of the immensity of their numbers.

Daniel (vii. 10) says: "Thousands on thousands minis-tered to Him, and ten hundred times a hundred thousand assisted before His throne".

The *Apocalypse* (v. 11): "And their numbers were thousands on thousands".

Job (xxv. 3): "Whether is there a limit to the number of His soldiers".

There is a fitness in the multitudes of the heavenly hosts. (1) God created beings to be happy around Him. His omnipotence and His beneficence would not be expressed by a scanty number. The vaster and more incalculable their numbers, the greater the manifestation of His power and His blessedness. (2) It is written in *Proverbs* (xiv. 28): "In the multitude of his people lieth the glory of the king, the ignominy of the prince in the scantiness of his nation". (3) If we make a computation of all the members of the human race from Adam till the last man, the numbers will all but pass beyond the reckoning of human figures. What reason is there that the angels should be less in number?

Bossuet (*1re Elevat.*) says: "Count, if you can, the sands on the seashore; count, if you can, the stars in the firmament, those that you can see, as well as those that you cannot; and when you have done so, be firmly convinced that you have not yet reached the number of the angels; for, point out to me what is most perfect in heaven or on earth, and on that, I say, does God most lavishly outpour the abundance of His omnipotence and His love".

"Prodigality　　　　is a characteristic of all the divine works.　　　　We cannot meditate on the countless multitudes of the angels without astonishment. So vast a populace, of such surpassing beauty, of such gigantic intelligence, of such diversified nature, is simply overwhelming to our most ambitious thoughts. A locust-swarm, and each locust an archangel; the myriads of points of life disclosed to us by the microscope, and each point a grand spirit; the sands of the seas and the waters of the ocean, and each grain and each drop a beautiful being, the brightness of whose substance we could not see and live : this is but an approximation to the reality. So theologians teach us." —Faber, *Precious Blood*, p. 223.

6. *Question.*—Are the angels all of one species?

Answer.—The angels are not all of one species. Scripture frequently speaks of distinctions and differences; some angels, some archangels, &c. Theologians generally teach that different gifts of grace have been bestowed on the angels, marking out, therefore, different capacities, *i.e.*, different species. St. Dionysius, writing on the heavenly hierarchy, says : "The sacred volumes declare that these holy superior beings differ from one another by different grades". St. Jerome, writing against Jovinian : "Among the invisible creatures there is a manifold and an indefinite diversity". St. Augustine and St. Anselm teach the same. Reason would tell us, if we look at bird differing from bird, beast from beast, flower from flower, tree from tree, that the variety of the species enhances the beauty and harmony of the creation. The same way is it with the beautiful angels in heaven.

7. *Question.*—Are there many individuals in each species?

Answer.—The great St. Thomas would have it that there is only one angel of every species, thus showing forth the magnificence of the designs and the perfection of this wonderful work of God. This is not the opinion commonly held, however; nearly all the rest of the schoolmen hold the opposite opinion. St. Augustine (in his *Enchiridion* 29) finds an unanswerable argument in the fact of the condemnation of the angels; for, he says, "if each angel constituted a separate and distinct species, then numerous, separate, and distinct species were condemned to hell, and lost absolutely and for ever to heaven, which can hardly be thought of; whereas, if there were several individuals of each species, there would still be representatives of each species in heaven".

With our notions of things earthly, it appears rather to harmonise that there should be many members of each species, than that each angel should constitute a distinct species.

Cardinal Newman, in his *Grammar of Assent* (47), without, however, giving any adhesion to the doctrine, says: "The angels have been considered by divines to have each of them a species to himself, and we may fancy each of them so absolutely *sui similis* as to be like nothing else".

Father Faber, in his work *All for Jesus* (p. 160), says very beautifully: "Scripture teaches us a great deal about the angels, their worship of God, their ministries towards other creatures, their individual characters, as in the case of Michael, Gabriel, and Raphael, their multitude and their nine choirs by name. Some theologians have thought that each angel is a species of himself, which would, indeed, open out quite an overwhelming view of the magnificence of God. Others, *with more show of reason*, make twenty-seven species, three in each choir, as there are three choirs in each hierarchy ; and even this gives us amazing ideas of the court of heaven, when we remember how hard it is for us to conceive of any further specific division of reasonable creatures than into those with bodies and those purely spiritual."

8. The natural life of the angels.

We know what the natural life of man consists in : he breathes, his heart beats, his blood circulates, he eats and drinks, he sleeps and walks about, he thinks, reasons, acts. Now, in what does the life, the natural life, of the angels consist? In four things : in the exercise of the intellect, the exercise of the will, the interchange of thought, and the power of acting. This is the teaching of divines.

The angels, by the natural powers belonging to them as angels, can know God, can know themselves, one another, and, finally, the soul of man. They know God. God was their first beginning, their last end, and this knowledge was the primary and chief object to which the powers of their intellect were to be turned. They know themselves. That is simply what we understand by being alive. They know the other angels, as being fellow-citizens of the heavenly city. They know the human soul, as forming a portion, like themselves, of God's vast creation.

9. *Question.*—Can the angels know, and do they know, all the material things of this world?

Answer.—Yes ; they know all the material world. They know the mineral world and all its properties, such as geology, for example, teaches, but in an indefinitely higher degree than geologists know it. They know the vegetable world and all its varied and different properties also, flowers, and shrubs, and trees, and vegetables, and mosses. They know the firmament world—all that astronomy teaches about the sun and the stars, their motions, their orbits, their substances. They know all about the animal world, and its equally diversified creatures, their formation, their habits, modes of life, &c., from the microscopic animalcula to the lord of the creation—man. God gave them this knowledge, and it may be said of them that if they did not know these things at one glance, they would have a curiosity (as being members of creation) to know these things which formed other parts of the same creation as they were.

10. *Question.*—Do the angels know future things?

Answer.—The angels know some, not all, future things; they know those things which necessarily follow from natural causes. But the things which are merely accidental in the future, or those necessary consequences of natural causes which by God's providence, or otherwise, may be changed, they do not know. Let us take example of the foretelling of a storm, which an American paper appears to the unlearned to supernaturally predict. Now, an angel knows that a current of air is passing in the Western regions. It knows all the laws whereby the atmosphere is guided. It knows at what speed it is travelling. It knows at what time, with a certain rate of motion, it would reach a given place. As a rule, it could predict of it that it would do so by a certain period; men can do that much. Thus, to an extent, it can tell future things. But unforeseen causes may arise and interfere, and then it would not be infallible in its judgment. Suppose a person was sick, one of those mentioned in the Bible, and sick unto death, an angel from its super-human medical skill would predict its death. But in the meantime our Blessed Lord is entreated : He enters, and the disease flies at His approach ; then the angel would be mistaken in his calculation ; so speaks St. Thomas. But Suarez and others hold that the angels know what will eventually happen, provided these things depend upon necessary causes. This will be better understood by the following.

11. *Question.*—Can they know future things, not arising from necessary causes ?

Answer.—No ; for the knowledge of future things, that depend on free-will for their coming into being, is ever set down as the special mark of the Divinity.

"Tell what shall happen in the future, and we will know that ye are gods" (*Isaias* xli. 23).

"I am God, and there is no one like Me, telling from the beginning the latest thing to happen, and from the commencement the things that have not yet begun to be" (*Isaias* xlix. 9).

St. Hilary says: "What is so peculiar to God as the knowledge of the future?"

St. Hilary: "To no one else but to One, and that One God, does it belong to know the future".

Tertullian: "The truth of divination I hold to be the distinct testimony of the Divinity".

This is important, as it leads us to understand what is the knowledge of the demons, and whether they can foretell future things, which do not happen by fixed laws; as, for instance, when the oracle was asked, "Shall Pyrrhus conquer the Romans?" the oracle did not know. The answer it gave was ambiguous. It made reply: "The Romans Pyrrhus shall conquer"—which might mean that Pyrrhus would conquer the Romans, or the Romans would conquer Pyrrhus. Hence Cicero says: "Their divinations were partly false, partly true," as may happen to any one; oftener still ambiguous so as to square with any event; and, therefore, their responses were generally despised by the more learned and keener-minded of the heathens, as Origen and Eusebius testify. The Roman general had little confidence in the sacred chickens. On an occasion, when before a battle they refused to take their food, he flung them into the sea, with the exclamation: "If they do not eat let them drink". This, however, lost him the battle, for the soldiers, thinking it a bad omen, got so disheartened that they easily yielded to the enemy.

12. *Question.*—Can the angels know for a certainty free acts of the intellect and the will either in other angels or in man?

Answer.—No, not without the consent of the others. God alone can do so.

Scripture says: "God searches all hearts, and understands all the thoughts of the mind. Thou alone (O Lord) knowest the heart of man" (*Paralip.* xxviii. 9).

"Wicked and inscrutable is the heart of all; *who shall understand it? I, the Lord,* searching the hearts and reins" (*Jerem.* xvii. 17).

St. Hilary: "The thoughts of the heart it is not ours to

know, but His, of whom it is written : God, searching the reins and hearts ".

St. Ambrose : " When the Lord wished to save men, He showed that He was God, *by His knowledge of hidden things*".

St. Chrysostom : " But that you may know *it belongs to God alone to know the secrets of hearts,* hear what the Prophet says : ' Thou alone knowest hearts ' ".

This is the feeling that God's own hand has implanted in our minds, namely, that our thoughts should not be read by every passer-by, but only by those we wish, and according as we ourselves would reveal them. We would even conceal them, if possible, from God. From this it follows that the devil, when he tempts us, can only guess at what is going on in our minds. He cannot know for certain, except from our own outward manifestations, how we receive his suggestions, and whether we yield to them or not.

13. *Question.*—Are the mysteries of faith, as, for instance, the dogma of the Holy Trinity, as much beyond the natural powers of the angels to understand as beyond ours ?

Answer.—Just the same. They can no more of their own powers understand the great mysteries of faith, as they really are, no more than we can. They must bow their heads as we do, when reflecting on the Incarnation, the Blessed Eucharist, &c.

14. *Question.*—But in natural things that they can understand, is there a knowledge from inference in the angels, *i.e.,* knowing one thing do they conclude another ?

Answer.—No ; they see all natural things at one and the

most luminous glance. For instance, they know at one glance the essence of man's nature, all its properties, individual conditions, and so on; the same way with all the material world. And from this we are also to conclude that there is no such thing as being deceived with the angels in those things which come within their knowledge.

15. *Question.*—What is meant by the *morning* and *evening* knowledge of the angels?

Answer.—Divines distinguish two sources of knowledge in the angels: (1) By the Beatific Vision the angels see all things, present, past, future, and most perfectly, in God ; this is called the *morning* knowledge, because both of its priority and of its clearness.   (2) The angels afterwards see things as they really take place. This knowledge is not so noble, nor so perfect as the *morning*, and, therefore, because of its lateness and its dimness, is called the *evening* knowledge. St. Augustine, in his *City of God*, says : " The knowledge of a creature is (if I might use the expression) more discoloured than the knowledge of it as seen in God, just as art is less than the first principle—Nature ; and, therefore, very fittingly is that knowledge called *evening* knowledge ". St. Thomas says : " As of forenoon and afternoon a day is customarily made up, so of *morning* and *evening* science the days and knowledge of an angel ".   It is well to remember these two terms.

16. *Question.*—Can the angels desire, and love, and hate, or rejoice and sorrow ?

Answer.—These things are attributed to them in the

Scriptures, but none of these external things affect their substantial bliss and glory and happiness in the Beatific Vision.

17. *Question.*—Are the angels endowed naturally with free-will like man?

Answer.—Yes; the Scriptures everywhere speak of them as obeying the commands of God, as worthy of reward or punishment, and this could not be unless they had free-will.

The Holy Fathers.—St. Damascene says: "An angel is a being endowed with free-will, for everything that makes use of reason is also endowed with free-will"

St. Gregory Nyss.: "God ordained that whatsoever is honoured with reason and intelligence is ruled by free-will".

St. Fulgent: "God gave liberty to the angels, that their loyalty might have the approval of their will".

18. *Question.*—Are the angels of their own nature exposed to sin?

Answer.—Yes; the angels, not alone in their own nature, but even raised to a supernatural order and strengthened, therefore, by God's grace, did actually sin.

The Holy Fathers.—St. Jerome says: "It is God alone to whom sin cannot be imputed. All others, since they enjoy free-will, may turn that will to either side."

St. Ambrose: "Every creature, according to the capacity of his nature, receives the accidents of good and evil, and feels the same yielding to evil".

St. Augustine: "It is manifest that sin is destruction,

annihilation *(nihilum)*, and that men, when they sin, become *nothing*". Now, according to St. Thomas, "Every creature has this (of its nature) *to tend namely to nothing*, since *out of nothing* it was made"; therefore, to make use of the words of St. Augustine, in his *City of God*, "Every intellectual creature is mutable, *i.e.*, prone to sin, since *out of nothing it was made*".

Bossuet says: Some creatures, and they the most perfect, are drawn out of nothing, just as others; *and those*, all perfect though they be, *are exposed to sin.* One Being alone is by His own nature impeccable—He who is of Himself, and who by His essence is perfect. But, since He alone is perfect, it follows that everything besides is defective, according to holy Job: "And He hath found depravation even in His angels". Again, the rule directing angelic intelligence is by nature either intrinsic or extrinsic. If the former, the rule would be identified with the very nature of the actor, and could not therefore be deviated from; but if the latter, then it can. Now, the rule in the case of the angels (as well as in that of man) is the sovereign will of God, which is extrinsic, and which consequently may be deviated from; and hence angels may sin. To quote the words which the great bishop of Meaux addresses to a fallen angel: "Truly everything drawn out of nothing has still some of its belongings. You were sanctified, but not essentially holy as God. You were ruled at first before you fell (not as God, whose own will is His rule), but you were ruled by an indefectible sovereign will—the will of God."

To be naturally peccable it is sufficient that one can be drawn aside by any passion, as pride, envy, hatred; and also that one be free to follow or resist that passion. Now, that is what happened in the case of the angels.

19. *Question.*—Does not sin presuppose in the intellect a defect either of truth or of attention to that truth? and surely such could not be in the case of the angels.

Answer.—Generally, indeed, there is some defect, for it is hard to believe that an intellect, such as the angels', strongly and intently gazing on truth, could, without that defect, give way to sin; yet that is not absolutely impossible. But, an angel (speaking now only in the natural order) does not at every moment consider all the things it might consider; nor, again, does it consider all with equal attention, for this is the necessary consequence of the possession of free will; therefore it can fail in attention, and in will too. At any rate, it is certain that they, like us, possess (happily in one sense, unhappily in another) *the great gift of free will*, whereby they might obey or disobey, love or hate, the great Creator of all.

PART II.

THE EXCELLENCE OF THE ANGELS.

20. *Question.*—Can the angels converse with one another, and how?

Answer.—The angels speak one to another. The Scripture uses the same word of their conversation that it does to designate human speech : "The Seraphim cried out one to another and said, Holy, holy, holy, Lord God of

Sabaoth " (*Isa.* vi. 3); "If I should speak with the tongues of men and of angels" (1. *Cor.* xiii. 1); "When Michael, the archangel, was disputing with the devil, he said, The Lord command thee" (*Epis. Jude* i. 9); and so all the Fathers.

The angels, therefore, can speak to God. They praise His power, they extol His majesty, they beseech His clemency, they consult His wisdom. Thus, it is related in *Zachary*, the angel replied to God, and said: "Lord of Armies, how long wilt thou not have mercy on Jerusalem and the cities of Juda?" (i. 12). In the book of *Job*, Satan is introduced many times as speaking to God.

In like manner, the angels can speak to men, as the archangel Gabriel to the Blessed Virgin. St. Thomas, and with him the generality of theologians, are of opinion that though angels can speak of their own natural powers, yet, in communication with themselves there is no need to make use of words, but that God has so made them that mind speaks to mind. This, too, seems more noble, and more in accordance with our notions of the angels.

"Cast your eye over that outspread ocean, whose shores lie so faintly and far off in the almost infinite distance. It gleams like restless silver, quivering with one life, and yet such multitudinous life. It flashes in the light with intolerable magnificence. Its unity is numberless. Its life is purest light. Into the bosom of its vastness the glory of God shines down, and the universe is illuminated with its refulgence. It is an ocean of life. Who can count the sum of being that is there? Who but God can fathom its unsearchable caverns? What created eye but is dazzled with the blazing splendour of its capacious surface? It breaks upon its shores in mighty waves; and yet there is no sound. Grand storms of *voiceless* praise hang over it for ever, storms of ecstatic lightning without any roll of thunder, *whose very silence* thrills the souls of the human saints, and is one of their celestial joys—*that deep stillness* of unsounding worship. This is the world of angels."—F. Faber, *Precious Blood*, p. 140.

21. *Question.*—What is the power of the angels with regard to this visible creation?

Answer.—The power of the angels is immense. The Scriptures ascribe to them the destruction of Sodom and Gomorrah, the destruction of Sennacherib's army, and of the firstborn of the Egyptians; and to the bad angels, Job's afflictions, the destruction of his goods, and the death of his children; the possession of men (as in the New Testament); the rushing of the herd of swine into the sea, &c. Thus also of Antichrist, the principal minister of Satan, miraculous things are foretold in the Apocalypse.

We cannot exactly define how great is their power. This, however, we know, that they cannot contravene any of the divine or natural laws, or even the physical laws of the globe, —that their power is entirely subject to the wish and permission of Almighty God, "otherwise the evil spirits could any day overturn the entire world" (Bonal, *De Angelis*). Later on this matter will be treated more fully; here it is sufficient to say that they can produce most wonderful effects, as exciting storms and tempests, striking the earth with interior motions, causing foul dreams and diseases, or sometimes curing sickness and wounds, and bringing about

health in man or beast, when it pleases God to allow them
to do so. In that enchanting little gem, the *Dream of
Gerontius,* when the departed soul is approaching the judg-
ment-seat, it thus converses with its guardian angel :

SOUL.
But hark! upon my sense
Comes a fierce hubbub, which would make me fear,
Could I be frighted?

ANGEL.
We are now arrived
Close on the judgment court; that sullen howl
Is from the demons who assemble there.
It is the middle region, where of old
Satan appeared among the sons of God,
To cast his gibes and scoffs at holy Job.
So now his legions throng the vestibule,
Hungry and wild to claim their property,
And gather souls for hell.   Hist to their cry !

SOUL.
How sour and how uncouth a dissonance !

ANGEL.
It is the restless panting of their being ;
Like beasts of prey, who, caged within their bars,
In a deep hideous purring have their life,
And an incessant pacing to and fro.

SOUL.
How impotent they are ! and yet on earth
They have repute for wondrous power and skill ;
And books describe, *how that the very face
Of the Evil One, if seen, would have a force
Even to freeze the blood, and choke the life
Of him who saw it.*

ANGEL.
In thy trial-state
Thou hadst a traitor nestling close at home,
Connatural, who with the powers of hell

Was leagued, and of thy senses kept the keys,
And to that deadliest foe unlocked thy heart.
And therefore is it, in respect of man,
Those fallen ones show so majestical.
But when some child of grace, angel or saint,
Pure and upright in his integrity
Of nature, meets the demons on their raid,
They scud away as cowards from the fight.
Nay, oft hath holy hermit in his cell,
Not yet disburdened of mortality,
Mocked at their threats and warlike overtures ;
Or dying, when they swarmed, like flies around,
Defied them, and departed to his Judge.

22. *Question.*—Are angels superior to man ?

Answer.—The natural excellence of the angels far surpasses that of man.

The Scriptures say : "Thou hast found him a little less
than the angels" (*Ps.* viii. 6). This text in its mystical
sense is used of Christ, but in its literal historic sense is
made use of with regard to man. Of the demon it is said :
"There is not a power on earth could compare with him"
(*Job* xli. 24). St. Augustine, in his *City of God*, says : "The
angelic world in its natural dignity surpasses all other things
that the Lord has made" ; and from its very excellence, he
argues : "By so much was their transgression the more cul-
pable, by as much as their dignity was the more sublime".
Even the very gentile races believed in their superiority, and
also in their power to injure or serve, and hence they paid
to them an inferior worship, as beings to be propitiated.

23. *Question.*—Whether, during their time of trial, did
the angels receive supernatural grace ?

Answer.—Yes; all the angels received grace from God during their time of trial.

(1) The good angels received it. They were created for eternal blessedness just as man, and grace is as necessary for them in order to obtain supernatural merit as for man; therefore they received supernatural grace.

St. Basil says: "There is no sanctification without the Spirit; for not even the Virtues of heaven were of their own nature sanctified: if that were the case, there would then, indeed, be no difference between them and the Holy Ghost". Didymus, in his first book on the *Holy Spirit*, says: "The Holy Ghost not alone accompanies (as Indweller) men who are far away from heaven, but even does so with each and every one of the angels". St. Damascene: "By a word the angels were created, and by the *sanctification of the Holy Ghost* they have received all manner of perfection".

(2) The bad angels received grace; for the same is asserted of them as of the good angels, and the Scriptures and the Fathers strongly emphasise the fact.

Isaias: "How art thou fallen from heaven, O Lucifer, who didst arise as the morning?" These words mean a fall from a place of eminent dignity and excellence, such as the wonderful brightness and splendour of the grace of God. No natural brightness of the angels, great though it be, is like to it.

Ezechiel (xxviii. 12): "Thou wast the seal of remembrance, *full of wisdom, and perfect in beauty*. Thou wast in the pleasures of the paradise of God—every precious stone thy covering, the sardius, the topaz, and the jasper, the chrysolite, and the onyx, and the berl, the sapphire, and the carbuncle, and the emerald—gold the work of thy beauty; and thy pipes were prepared in the day thou wast created. Thou a cherurbim, stretched out and protecting, and I set thee in the holy mountain of God, thou hast walked in the midst of the stones of fire. Thou wast perfect in thy ways from the day of thy creation until iniquity was found in thee." The Holy Fathers, in commenting on these words of Ezechiel, apply them to Lucifer, although, in the sacred text, the words are historically addressed to the King of Tyre. Writing on "thou wast the seal of remembrance," they understand the phrase to signify that Lucifer was created with very great excellence to an exceeding close image of God; and the other words, "full of wisdom, perfect in beauty," are always used in Scripture as the perfection of supernatural grace. Our Blessed Lord Himself says of the demon: "He was a murderer, and stood not in the truth " (*John* viii. 44). Now, by the word "truth" in this text, St. Thomas and the Fathers, especially the Greek Fathers, understand "grace" The same is said in other words in the epistle of *St. Jude* (in the 6th verse): "And the angels who kept not their principality, but forsook their own habitation, He hath reserved under darkness in everlasting chains ".

Man, as is commonly held, was created in the state of grace; now, it was fitting that angels, too, should be created in a state of grace, since the end for which man and angels were created was the same; since, moreover, the angels' nature was more perfect, and, therefore, ought not to be longer deprived of the grace of sanctification; and since, especially, all of God's works are perfect, and ought not, therefore, to be less so in the case of angels than of men.

24. *Question.*—But did they receive sanctifying grace at the instant of their creation?

Answer.—Most probably, and all but certainly, yes.

St. Augustine says: "God created the angels, building up in them their nature, *and at the same time* bestowing on them His grace".

St. Basil: "The angels were not created *in a weakling state,* by degrees increasing and growing perfect, and thus become worthy of the reception of the Spirit; but in their very formation, and as if mixed with their substance, *they received at the instant of creation the infusion of grace*".

St. Bonaventure, discussing the matter, thus writes: "It is to be answered that this is a question of fact; and since there is nothing else to guide us than the congruity of God's doing so, we may regard both opinions as probable, like others before us. Some say that the angels were created in grace, and they argue from God's liberality and the angels' fitness that it must be so: God being willing to give where no obstacle is placed, and the angels being pure and clear vessels offering no obstacle to the infusion of His grace; so that God did not leave them empty (as it were) even for a moment, but the instant He created them that instant He enriched them. They find an analogy in His creation of the inanimate world: the trees He brought forth clothed with verdure and laden with fruit; equally so all other things in their highest and noblest state, and hence they infer the angels in the enjoyment of grace.

"Others, however, there are who hold that the angels did not receive grace at the first instant, but afterwards. They argue that though God could do as the supporters of the other opinion say, yet His liberality is regulated according to wisdom and justice. For instance, God could have redeemed man immediately after his fall ; it would appear to have been more liberal than what He did, yet He did not. Then it were more fitting (they say) that the angels, seeing how good the grace of God was, should covet it and thus receive it. According to this view Lucifer never had grace ; and if he, who was the highest amongst them, had it not, *a fortiori* the others had it not. This opinion the Master of the Sentences [Scotus] seems to accept, and indeed it may be looked upon as the more generally accepted of the two. It is further argued by them that the angels' conversion must take place from some indifferent standpoint ; from this the good angels were converted to good and therefore deserved merit, the wicked to evil and were therefore condemned."

This is no longer the common opinion. Modern theologians find it under every sense more convenient to hold that God created the angels from the very first in a state of grace, that He then placed a labour or trial before them— what that trial was will be discussed later on—that the wicked angels failed in the endurance of that trial, and their sin was therefore doubly malicious ; that the good angels were faithful, and stepped from grace to greater grace, and to the enjoyment of the Beatific Vision.

" Each angel, perhaps, had thousands of beautiful graces. To many of these we on earth could give no name, if we beheld them. But they were all wonderful, all instinct with supernatural holiness and spiritual magnificence."— F. Faber, *Precious Blood*, p. 15.

And again : "God became a King by becoming a Creator. It was thus He gained an empire over which His insatiable love might rule. Nature is very beautiful, whether we think of angelic or human nature. Created Nature is a shadow of the Uncreated Nature, so real and so bright that we cannot think of it without exceeding reverence. *Yet God created neither angels nor man in a state of nature.* This is, to my mind, the most wonderful and the most suggestive thing which we know about God. He would have no reasonable nature, even from the very first, which should not be partaker of His Divine Nature. This is the very meaning of a state of grace. He, as it were, clung to His creation while He let it go. He would not leave it to breathe for one instant in a merely natural state. The very act of creation was full of the fondness of maternal jealousy. It was, to speak in a human way, as if He feared that it would wander from Him, and that His attractions would be too mighty for the littleness of finite beings. Oh, that majesty of God, which seems clothed with such worshipful tranquillity in the eternity before creation, how passionate, how yearning, how mother-like, how full of inventions and excesses it appears in the act of creation."—*Idem.*, p. 85.

25. *Question.*—What mysteries of faith did the angels know explicitly during their probation ?

Answer.—(1) *The unity of God,* and all those attributes which belong to the unity of God, as, for instance, that He is the Sanctifier, and that He is the great Rewarder; according to St. Paul: "For he that cometh to God must believe that *He is*, and *is a Rewarder* to those that seek Him" (*Heb.* xi. 6). In order to love God above all things it is necessary that we must have supernatural faith, for how else could we have hope in Him, or how else could we look to Him as the object of eternal blessedness; therefore the angels had such supernatural faith. Also, during their time of trial, the angels understood all those truths which natural reason teaches regarding God, as the Creator, the Supreme Lord, the First Truth, &c.

(2) The angels knew by divine revelation the mystery of the Sacred Trinity, and believed in it—such is the common opinion held by theologians—and that the angels understood it much more distinctly than we do. Even the Prophets of the Old Law, it is believed, knew of the Trinity.

"In the Old Testament there is not, indeed, that express mention of the Holy Trinity which is to be found in the New; either because there was danger of the Jews being led to believe there were more Gods than one, or because God wished by little and little to lead the weakness of man's intellect to the knowledge of the highest and most inconceivable mysteries; yet are there many passages where vestiges of the Sacred Trinity are to be found, nor are there wanting testimonies from which it may be gathered there are several Persons in God" (Delahogue). He quotes in proof the following :—

"Let *us* make man to our *own* image" (*Gen.* i.).

"Behold Adam is become as *one of ourselves*" (*Gen.* iii.).

At the Tower of Babel : "Come, let us descend, and

confound their tongues"; on which St. Chrysostom says: "Behold, I beseech you, how the voice of the Father calls on the Son and the Holy Spirit; it is the voice of one addressing two equals".

St. Thomas says that the essential beatitude of the angels [*i.e.*, after their term of probation] consists in the intuitive vision of the Divine Essence. Now, the Divine Essence, as it is in itself, cannot be seen without the Three Divine Persons also; "Therefore," Suarez argues, "an explicit faith in that mystery [during the term of probation] ought to be required as a necessary means to salvation".

Arguing from what is required in man, viz., an explicit faith in the Sacred Trinity, both in man's fallen state and in the Christian Dispensation, we conclude that it was required also in the angels. It was not required under the Old Dispensation, but that was because of the imperfection of the Old Dispensation—an imperfection which is not to be attributed to the state of the angels.

(3) It is most probable the angels knew of the mystery of the Incarnation by divine revelation, and believed in it. St. Thomas among the elder Schoolmen, and the great Suarez among the modern, are the leaders in the opinion which holds that the bad angels fell because of this wonderful act of divine condescension. They desired the hypostatic union for themselves, and envied it to man.

"The *mystery* of the kingdom of God, *which is fulfilled in Christ our Lord, all the angels, indeed, knew of from the beginning* in some qualified way; but chiefly those who were made blessed, confirmed by the vision of the Word—a vision which the demons never had" (St. Thomas). St.

Paul says : " And again, when He bringeth in the First-Begotten into the world, He says, And let all the angels of God adore Him " (*Heb.* i. 6). It was therefore fitting for the glory and honour of the Son of God who was to come in human flesh that the angels should know this mystery. Moreover, Christ is the head of the angels, and the angels His ministers, and therefore it was proper that from the commencement they should acknowledge Him as their Lord and Master.

26. *Question.*—Did the angels know this mystery fully with all its circumstances and details ?

Answer.—It is believed they did not. Most likely the angels during probation knew it only in an obscure way. Just as it was one of the first things told by God to Adam, and he then had an undefined knowledge of it as a future event which God would bring about in His own way. Adam, however, knew that the Redeemer was to be born of woman. So, too, the angels. St. Thomas says they did not know all the circumstances relating to Redemption. But after probation it is believed the angels knew this sacred mystery ; and not to mention their knowledge by reason of the Beatific Vision, they knew it partly before Christ, partly after, either by the will and revelation of God, or by the prophecies, or, finally, by seeing the acts of Christ Himself, and by the teaching of the Apostles, according to the saying of St. Paul : " To me, the least of all the saints, is given the grace to preach   in order that the manifold wisdom of God may be made known to the Principalities and Powers in the heavenly places, through the Church, according to the eternal purpose, which He made in Christ Jesus our Lord" (*Eph.* iii. 10).

Father Faber thus speaks of their knowledge of the Precious Blood during their term of probation: "The angels wonder more than men, because they better understand it. Their superior intelligence ministers more abundant matter to their love. From the very first he invited the angels to adore it. He made their adoration a double exercise of humility—of humility towards Himself, and of humility towards us, their fellow creatures. It was the test to which He put their loyalty. He showed them His beloved Son, the Second Person of the Holy Trinity, in His Sacred Humanity, united to a lower nature than their own, and in that lower nature crowned their King and Head to be worshipped by them with absolute and unconditional adoration. The Son of a human mother was to be their Head, and that daughter of Eve to be herself their Queen. He showed them in that Blood the source of all their graces. Each angel, perhaps, had thousands of beautiful graces yet there was not a single grace in any angel which was not merited for him by the Blood of Jesus, and which had not also its type and counterpart in that Precious Blood. The Precious Blood, man's Blood, was as the dew of the whole kingdom of the angels. It would have redeemed them, had they needed to be redeemed, or were they allowed to be redeemed. But as it was not so, it merited for them, and was the source of, all their graces. Well, then, may the angels claim to sing the song of the Lamb; to whose outpoured Human Life they also owed so much, though not because it was outpoured."—*Precious Blood*, p. 15.

It is to be understood that the angels did not clearly know or see God during their time of trial, and the reason is, "because this knowledge is the *primum premium*, which being attained, the soul rests blessed and happy" (Bonaventure).

Not even in heaven will the angels know God as He really is. The most blessed Soul of our Lord Jesus Christ, great and wonderful as it is, will not know the Divine Essence fully and entirely. To do so, an intelligence should be as infinite as God Himself. No created intelligence is infinite, and, therefore, the human Soul of our Blessed Lord, insomuch as it is a created thing, cannot know God fully and entirely as He is.

St. Bonaventure says: "The good angels had no foreknowledge during their time of trial that they would remain faithful, nor had the wicked any of their fall; if such were not the case a twofold inconvenience would arise. First, if God gave to the good angels a foreknowledge of their remaining faithful, then the devil might excuse himself that he did not get a knowledge that was vouchsafed to others; and secondly, if a foreknowledge of their fall was disclosed to the wicked, then they were left without hope and tempted to their ruin; and, furthermore, the pain begotten of such knowledge would be unjustly inflicted by God, inasmuch as it was inflicted before they had committed any evil. To none, therefore, of the angels (he concludes) was their future lot revealed."

27. *Question.*—Did the angels, while in a state of probation, elicit acts meriting future glory?

Answer.—Yes; just as men on earth elicit meritorious acts, so did they.

The Scripture says : " No one is crowned except he who has legitimately striven " (2 *Tim.* ii. 5) ; and in *Proverbs* xii. 14 : " To each one there shall be given according to the work of his hands ". This is the law of God, not alone for men, but for angels also.

The Holy Fathers.—Pope Gelasius says " That the angels were so constituted as to merit an increase of eternal glory is sufficiently indicated by the fact that, had they stood in need of nothing more, then none of them could have committed evil ".

St. Prosper, writing on the contemplative life, says : " It was the action of the will of the holy angels, that while their companions with their own free-will fell, they themselves remained in the dignity wherein God had placed them ; and hence it came to pass, by a divine and a most just judgment, that what was only up to that a holy desire of remaining with their God, became thereafter a voluntary and most blessed necessity of remaining with Him for evermore "

Argument from Reason.—The angels, good and bad, were placed in an equal condition with regard to merit and demerit. Now, the wicked angels had the power of demeriting, and did demerit ; therefore the good angels had the power of meriting, and did merit. Again, it is more perfect to have a thing from one's own act than to owe it absolutely to another ; therefore, since all God's works are perfect—namely, of meriting by their own acts—the angels had that perfection. How long the state of probation lasted we do not know; but this seems to be the order of the angels' acts   first, by a free act (as in the case, for instance, of adults being baptised) they received with all their reason and will sanctifying grace; secondly (placed in that state of sanctifying grace), they were then in a position to earn supernatural merit, and while in that position, as all the Holy Fathers and the Theologians teach, they were still *viatores* (*travellers, i.e.,* not as yet confirmed), and as such that they elicited acts deserving of supernatural reward. "Consequently, according to almost all, that subsequent act, by which an increase of grace and glory was merited, was, in a way, a distinct act from the first act, and *corresponding to several instants of our time,* and coexisting with several acts which had been ordered [them by God], and which were *successive* in the angels themselves" (Bonal).

28. *Question.*—Did the angels, who were more excellent by nature, receive more grace, merit, and glory than the others who were not so excellent?

Answer.—Yes; that is the common opinion of the Fathers and the Theologians.

St. Basil says: "The angels received their measure of sanctification according to the proportion by which they exceeded one another".

St. Damascene: "The angels, each according to his dignity and class, were made sharers of light and glory"; and the Fathers take this doctrine from St. Dionysius, who says he learned it from St. Paul: "*De Coelo Hier.*"

Argument from Reason.—The angelic nature had been created by God for the purpose of receiving grace and enjoying blessedness; and as there were different choirs and different orders of spirits, and as variety adds to the beauty of a work, so was it fitting that there should be among the angels different degrees of grace and merit and glory, just as there is amongst men, or just as a builder in raising a house will dress some portions of it more elaborately than others.

Care must be taken however not to confound *efficacious grace* with the graces of which we have been speaking. God made no position or class of angels which should necessarily demand from His bounteous hand efficacious grace, or be necessarily denied it, because of its individual position or class.

29. *Question.*—What was the degree of grace and merit, and therefore of glory in the angels?

Answer.—Nothing more definite can be said than, as St. Thomas puts it, that it was " intensely great, both by reason of the supremely excellent nature of the angels, and because God always increases and multiplies whatever is good ".

In comparing their grace with that of man, and excepting our Blessed Lady alone, it may be said that it is immensely greater than among the saints. The Blessed Virgin is placed beyond all; as the Church on the day of her assumption proclaims, " she is exalted above the choirs of angels in the heavenly kingdom "; and hence Suarez is of opinion that perhaps there is no other except the Blessed Virgin, or at least very few among the children of men, that can be compared with (at any rate) the supreme angels in their perfection of grace and glory.

Here we have to adore the liberality of Almighty God and the mysterious and adorable way in which He distributes His gifts.   First, He fashions the angels in a natural order, and in that natural order He endows some with greater natural perfection than others according to the ideal in the Divine Mind from eternity.   Next, He raises these angels in the first instant of creation to a supernatural order by the gift of sanctifying grace.   Then comes the time of probation, and after that term He confirms the good angels for ever in glory, and bestows on them the Beatific Vision and happiness and enlightenment and splendour, according to their own acts truly, but still more in proportion to the natural powers and dignity and excellence His own divine hand had bountifully bestowed on them from the beginning.   Here indeed was the potter and the potter's clay spoken of by St. Paul.   To man He acts differently.   Not in proportion to His natural excellence, to the powers of His mind, or to the outward gifts of His body does He reward him ; but " the foolish things of this earth hath God selected that He might confound the wise, and the weak things to confound the strong, that no flesh may glory to itself in His sight ".   And yet some of those weak things and those foolish things God has placed in an equality with—nay, even beyond—the brilliant angels, who never knew the weakness and the foolishness of our earthly nature.

30. *Question.*—When did the angels come into the possession of the Beatific Vision ?

Answer.—Before the resurrection of our Blessed Lord ? Yes ; for our Blessed Lord says (*Matt.* x. 10) : " Their angels

always see the Father's face ". All the Fathers understand
this of the Beatific Vision. Now, Christ says this of the
angel guardians, " *who have but the last place in the heavenly
hierarchy* " (Bonal) ; and therefore by much more reason is
it to be understood of the higher angels.

Before Christ's coming? Yes; for Daniel says: "Thousands on thousands ministered to Him and stand before
Him "; and in *Tobias* we read: " I am the Angel Raphael,
one of the seven who stand before the throne of God ".

Before the fall of man? Yes; for Satan was then a fallen
angel, and condemned when he tempted our first parents ;
and from that we construe that the unfallen angels were then
confirmed in glory, for, according to St. Thomas, " God is
quicker to reward than to punish ".

All theologians are agreed that " after the shortest delay,
taking into account their opportunity for meriting, and God's
decrees in their regard, the angels were confirmed in eternal
glory ".

"The beautiful life of the angels in heaven, God's eldest-
born, may also furnish us with ample materials for intercession, and our Lord seems to call our attention to it when He
bids us pray that we may do His holy will on earth as the
angels in heaven.

"Sister Minima of Gesu Nazareno, a Carmelite nun, who
lived at the time of the French invasion of Italy, and spent
a life of incessant and wonderful intercession, used continually to offer to the Divine Majesty the love of the first
choir of seraphim, in reparation for all the outrages then
going on in the world.

"It is remarkable, when we come to think of it, that

neither angels nor men were created in a state of nature, but in a state of grace, and were thus able at once to love God and to merit eternal life, which is nothing else than eternal society with Him. Grace was a better position than nature for loving God. By grace He could communicate Himself to us supernaturally. By it He at once got more love from us, and made us more able to love Him. Oh, that we had the hearts to take this in, and all that it involves! If we are come to weights and measures with infinite goodness, surely His love of us should be our measure of love of Him—a measure to which we must never cease to aspire, though we shall never attain it.

Well might St. Francis run about the woods in the valley of Spoleto: 'Oh! God not known! God not loved!' Well might St. Bruno cause the mountain solitudes to echo with his one life-long cry—'Oh! goodness! goodness! goodness!' Well might our dearest Lord appear to St. Gertrude, pale, weary, bleeding, and dust-stained, and say, 'Open your heart, my daughter, for I want to go in and lie down: I am weary of these days of sin '.

" But at last as we grow in the knowledge of God, we grow in His love also."—F. Faber, *All for Jesus,* p. 160 *et seq.*

PART III.

THE FALL OF THE ANGELS.

31. Milton, in his *Paradise Lost,* introduces Satan thus addressing the Sun :

" O thou, that with surpassing glory crowned
  Look'st from thy sole dominion, like the god
  Of this new world ; at whose sight all the stars
  Hide their diminished heads ; to thee I call,
  But with no friendly voice ; and add thy name,
  O Sun, to tell thee, how I hate thy beams
  That bring to my remembrance from what state
  I fell ; how glorious once, above thy sphere,
  Till pride, and worse ambition, threw me down,
  Warring in heaven against heaven's matchless King.
  Ah, wherefore ? He deserved no such return
  From me, whom He created what I was
  In that bright eminence.
                  Yet all His good proved ill in me
  And wrought but malice ; lifted up so high
  I 'sdained subjection, and thought one step higher
  Would set me highest, and in a moment quit
  The debt immense of endless gratitude.

  Oh ! had His powerful destiny ordained
  Me some inferior angel, I had stood
  Then happy ; no unbounded hope had raised
  Ambition ! Yet why not? Some other power
  As great might have aspired, and me, though mean,
  Drawn to his part ; but other powers, as great,
  Fell not, but stand unshaken, from within,
  Or from without, to all temptations armed.
  Hadst thou the same free will and power to stand?
  Thou hadst ; whom hast thou, then, or what t' accuse
  But heaven's free love dealt equally to all ? "

Prop.—Amongst the angels there were some who fell. This is of faith.

The Scripture says : " Amongst His angels He hath found wickedness " (*Job* iv. 18).

St. Peter says : " God did not spare His angels when they sinned " (2 *Peter* ii. 4).

Now these angels were not evil because of their nature,

for whatsoever is created by God cannot of itself be evil, but must be good; therefore it must be by their own free-will. The Council of Lateran says: "The devil and other demons were created by God, in their own nature, good, but they of themselves became evil". This was directed against the Manicheans.

32. *Question.*—What number of the angels fell?

Answer.—The number of the good angels, as well as of the bad, is alike unknown. We speak of the good angels vaguely as immense hosts, countless, and all but infinite in number. Now, of the fallen angels we can indubitably assert that an immense number of them fell. The saints say that an immense multitude of demons are constantly engaged tempting men, and working other evils. Thus also the Fathers. St. Damascene says: "There fell with Lucifer an immense multitude of angels subject to him".

33. *Question.*—Which was the greater number—those that persevered or those that fell?

Answer.—Those that persevered form far and away the greater number.

St. Thomas and the Schoolmen ground their opinion on the words of the *Apocalypse* xii. 4: "And the tail of the dragon drew down a third part of the stars of heaven".

St. Augustine, in his *City of God*, says: "Although the angels sinned, yet not all were filled with sin, when by far the greater number of good angels preserved the order of their nature in the heavens". The common teaching is, about a third of the angels fell.

34. *Question.*—Whether did God predestine man to fill the seats of the fallen angels ?

Answer.—Yes, according to the common opinion of the Holy Fathers.

St. Augustine says : " God collected, from the mortal race, disowned and justly condemned, a host of people by His grace, that He would fill up and restore that portion of the angels that had been lost; and thus that beloved and heavenly city would not be deprived of its due number of citizens, but, on the contrary, would be enriched by a more abundant number ".

St. Anselm " Wherefore we may safely say there will be people and generations of men on this earth, until the number of the angels be completed from men, and then the generations of men which take place in this life will cease" (*Tract. de Incarn.*, n. 208).

35. *Question.*— Were there fallen angels from every one of the different species or orders of angels ?

Answer.—It is more likely that angels fell from each species, although there are some who hold that it was only from the lesser grades there were defections.

Hugo says some fell from every grade.

Gregory says that men are assumed into every order of angels, and this would not be the case, unless angels fell from every order.

St. Bonaventure says : " Since Lucifer, who was of the highest order, fell, *multo fortius de aliis*".

The Scripture says : " Thou a cherub, until iniquity was found in thee " (*Ezech.* xxviii. 19).

St. Paul: "Neither death, nor angels, nor principalities, nor powers" (*Rom.* viii. 38).

St. Paul: "Our wrestling is against principalities and powers, against the rulers of this world of darkness, against the spirits of wickedness in the high places" (*Eph.* vi. 12).

St. Bonaventure says: "It is well to know, that since many in the higher and lesser grades stood firm, so also many fell from both. Among whom one was more excellent than all that fell; nor among those that remained firm was there one more dignified, as is shown by authority; for *Job* says: *He, the beginning of the ways of God;* and in *Ezechiel* we read: *Thou the seal of similitude, full of wisdom and perfect in beauty, thou wast in the delights of the paradise of God.* Gregory thus comments on these passages: ' By how much the more subtle in nature was he, by so much the more deeply was God's similitude impressed upon him '. Again, in *Ezechiel* it is written: *Every precious stone his covering:* that is, every angel was as if a garment to him; because, as Gregory says: ' He was far brighter than all the others '. And for this reason was he called Lucifer, as we read in Isaias: *How art thou fallen, O Lucifer, that didst arise as the morning!* And he is not to be taken as an *order,* but *as a single spirit,* who when he saw his own created eminence and perfection, grew proud towards his Creator, and desired to be equal to God, as is said in *Isaias: I will climb into heaven, and beyond the stars of heaven will I exalt my throne, for I will be like the Most High.* He desired to be like God, not by imitation, but by equality of power."

Thus we see that the fallen angels are not from one order, but from several at any rate.

It is remarkable that the names of seraphim, thrones, and dominations are never attributed in Scripture to the demons. It does not necessarily follow from this that out of these orders no angels fell, though one would be tempted to come to that conclusion. The reason is, these words so essentially mean heavenly attributes, as, for instance, seraphim, the ardour of love; thrones, the throne or dwelling of God; dominations, an excellency of dominion or will, peculiarly applicable to God, that they could not be predicated of demons in hell.

36. *Question.*—Are men, then, assumed into each thinned rank of angels?

Answer.—Yes. St. Thomas and Suarez say so. Here indeed is displayed the nobility of free-will and its unhappy fragility also; since in every order of rational beings some have turned it to good, purchasing therewith eternal kingdoms; some, on the other hand, unto evil, and incurring thereby eternal damnation.

37. *Question.*—Among the fallen angels was there one, sometimes called by the name of Lucifer, sometimes by the name of Satan or the adversary, sometimes by the name of devil or the accuser, who was the first to sin, and who then led the others to sin?

Answer.—Yes; according to the common opinion of the Holy Fathers and the Schoolmen.

The Scripture says: "He is king over all the children of pride" (*Job* xli. 25).

Lucifer is called "the prince of demons," and the demons

are called "his angels". "Depart from me, ye accursed, into everlasting fire, which was prepared for the devil and his angels" (*Matt.* xxv. 41).

"And there was a great battle in heaven : Michael and his angels fought with the dragon, and the dragon fought and his angels. And they prevailed not, neither was their place found any more in heaven. And that great dragon was cast out, that old serpent, who is called the devil and Satan, and he was cast into the earth, and his angels were thrown with him" (*Apoc.* xii. 7).

The Holy Fathers.—St. Eusebius says : "The first wicked spirit, who was also the cause of defection in the others, and who was the author of all wickedness, is called the dragon".

St. Ambrose : "The devil, with those angels whom he had drawn with him into his impiety, was cast down from the heights of heaven".

Lucifer, then, not alone by his example, but by his persuasion also, induced them to rebel.

38. *Question.*—Was Lucifer the first of all the angels in natural perfection ?

Answer.—Yes. Such is the opinion of those who hold that numbers fell from every one of the orders of angels.

The Scripture says : "How art thou fallen, O Lucifer, who didst arise as a star !" (*Isa.* xiv. 12).

"He is the beginning of the ways of God, who made him" (*Job* xl. 14).

The Holy Fathers.—St. Gregory, Pope, says : "Behemoth is called the beginning of the ways of God, for when God would create all things, He made him first of the angels, and more excellent than all the rest ".

Yet others say that he is not to be understood as standing out alone as the singularly excellent one, but that he was of the highest, inasmuch as none, at any rate, was higher than he. Bossuet says: " Holy and blessed spirits, who gave you strength against that proud spirit, that was one of the first of your princes, nay, perhaps, the very first of all ? "

St. Bonaventure asks the question : " Was Lucifer pre-eminent among the angels, and of the highest order ? And he answers by saying that such is the testimony of the saints and Scriptures ; and had he remained firm (he adds), he would have been placed in the first rank, for, *ad hoc haberet idoneitatem ex parte naturae.* He thus argues from reason : Lucifer desired to be lord over all, and believed that he could obtain it, so that he would be subject to none ; but this would hardly be probable, unless he saw that he exceeded all. He very beautifully answers an objection that may be put—viz., Would God permit His noblest creature thus to perish ?—by saying that in this is shown the wonderful justice of God, which observes so strict a balance that it will on no account disturb the established order, and will, because of sin, cast away those that it accounted most dear. Whence (he continues) I believe that so terrible a spectacle of divine severity was manifested in the case of the highest angel and the first man ; both of whom God moulded and decorated with His own hands, that we might learn how unalterably God hates sin, and especially pride, since for one movement of it in the heart the highest and noblest of his creation were cast into eternal punishment without hope and without cessation. From this we have to draw the conclusion that it is an awful thing to fall into the hands of the living God; and if God did not spare the noblest angel when he grew proud, what shall be the fate of a little dust and ashes when it dares to rebel?"

Milton, in his *Paradise Lost*, describing the assembling of the fallen angels, writes thus:

All these and more came flocking   . and now
Advanced in view, they stand, a horrid front
Of dreadful length, and dazzling arms in guise
Of warriors old, with ordered spear, and shield,
Awaiting what command their mighty chief
Had to impose: he through the armed files
Darts his experienced eye, and soon traverse
The whole battalion, views their order due,
Their visages and statures as of gods;
Their number last he scans.   And now his heart
Distends with pride.
          Far these beyond
Compare of mortal prowess, yet observed
Their dread commander; *he, above the rest,*
In shape and gesture proudly eminent,
Stood like a tower; his form had not yet lost
All her original brightness, nor appeared
Less than archangel ruined.
          But his face
Deep scars of thunder had intrenched, and care
Sat on his faded cheek, but under brows
Of dauntless courage and considerate pride,
Waiting revenge; cruel his eye, but cast
Signs of remorse and passion to behold
The fellows of his crime—the followers rather—
(Far other once beheld in bliss) condemned
For ever now to have their lot in pain.
Millions of spirits for his fault amerced
Of heaven, and from eternal splendours flung.

There was a lapse of time (*morula fuit*, St. Bonaventure) between the creation of the angels and their fall.

THE NATURE OF THE ANGELS' SIN.

39. *Question.*—What was the sin of Lucifer? Was it pride?

Answer.—Yes ; this is what theologians and ascetics unanimously teach.

Scripture says : " In pride all evil had its beginning " (*Job* iv. 14). " Thy pride dragged thee to hell. How art thou fallen, O Lucifer, that didst arise as the morning?— thou that saidst in thy heart, I will climb into heaven ; beyond the stars will I make my throne. I will be like the Most High " (*Isaias* xiv. 12). " He is king over all the children of pride " (*Job* xli. 25).

The Holy Fathers.—St. Augustine says : " Proud was that angel, and on that account envious : by that same pride was he led to turn from God and exalt himself; and by that very tyrannical habit he chose rather to lord it over subjects than to serve ". St. Ambrose says : " Whether in the fall of the angels, or in the sin of man, pride was the root of the evil ". St. Chrysostom : " What greater evil than pride ? Never had the devil been cast out of heaven, nor an angel turned into a demon, were it not for this iniquitous vice ".

Now, sin in general is an inordinate desire of, or complacency in, corporal pleasures, or riches, or one's own excellence, " the concupiscence of the flesh, the concupiscence of the eyes, and the pride of life". But earthly riches and corporal pleasures could offer no temptations to the angels, therefore their sin must be concupiscence of their own excellence—in other words, pride.

St. Bonaventure : " And hence as a just judgment for such pride, he was cast out of heaven (*id est de empyreo*), in which he had been placed ; and all those who had been partners of his sin were cast with him into darkness. For, as we read in the Apocalypse : *The dragon falling from heaven drew with him a third of the stars ;* because Lucifer, who was greater than the others, fell not alone, but many others fell with him who were consenting to his wickedness, and these falling downwards a dwelling of this outer darkness received. And this happened so for our probation that they would be a means of proving us. Hence the Apostle says : *Our wrestling is with the rulers of the world of this darkness against the spirits of wickedness in the high places,* because the demons who are spiritual and wicked dwell in this turbulent air, which is called *coelum,* that they might be near to trouble us ; and hence the devil is called *the prince of the air.* It is not given them to dwell in heaven (*in coelo*)—that were too blessed and happy ; neither on earth, lest they might persecute men too much ; but, according to Peter, in his canonical Epistle, they are placed in this darksome air ; they remain as in prison until the Day of Judgment. And then will they be cast into the infernal gulf, according as it has been written : ' Depart ye accursed into everlasting fire, which has been prepared for the devil and his angels '."

40. *Question.*—In what did the devil take pride ? What was the object of his pride ?

Answer.—All agree that the pride consisted in an inordinate desire to be like God. "I will be like the Most High"; but what one of God's attributes he particularly coveted is a matter of dispute. The following are the several opinions :—

(1) That he desired God's essence to be a deity—like and equal to God. "Thy heart was elevated in thy loveliness, and thou saidst : I am God ; and on the chair of God have I sat in the midst of the sea" (*Ezechiel* xxviii. 2). This opinion receives a strong corroboration from the fact of the first angel opposing Lucifer being called Michael : *Quis ut Deus?* (who is like to God ?) In this sense, however, it can hardly be accepted, for, as St. Thomas and the schoolmen say : How could an angel so lose its natural reason as not to see the absurdity and impossibility of this—that either he could be the equal of God, or that there could possibly be two Gods ? Even our human reason says that cannot be.

(2) That Lucifer could not bear the everlasting control of God ; that he too desired power, and subjects, and empire ; and that the attribute of God he thus "appetised" was His glorious sovereignty. St. Augustine and St. Thomas hold this ; and among the great writers and thinkers of the modern school, Bossuet inclines to it.

St. Bonaventure expounds this view : "The first sin of the angel was pride, which was *initiated in presumption, consummated in ambition, and confirmed in envy and hatred.* It was *initiated in presumption,* for as soon as he saw his own powers he *presumed ;* it was *consummated in ambition,* for, presuming in himself, he coveted that which was entirely beyond him, and which he never could attain. And this was confirmed in his turning away through envy

and hatred; because when he could not attain what he
desired, he began to be envious, and, through hatred, to
oppose what he had longed for. The wicked angel
coveted a likeness of God partly through *imitation* and
partly through *equivalence;* and this becomes apparent if
we look at what he coveted and in what way he coveted
it. The devil desired *to be lord over others,* and to
be so *by his own authority.* His desire to be lord over
others was a coveting of God's similitude by *imitation,* and
this he would have obtained had he remained faithful; but
to obtain it by his own authority, without merits and without a bestower, so that he would be subject to no one else
—this belonged to God alone, and in this he coveted a
similitude of equivalence. And this is what the holy writers
say; for Gregory declares he sought to be *sui juris*—
i.e., subject to no one else; Bernard, that he sought equality
of power; and Anselm, that he sought to rule without
deserving it.

"The lesser angels," he continues, "sinned by pride, not
in consenting to Lucifer, but in coveting excellence for
themselves. Their pride was conformable to the head of
all wickedness—viz., the prince of darkness. The demon
himself, attending to the strength and excellence of his
natural powers, wished to rule and rest on his own authority
—*i.e.,* without merits and without ministry. The demons
subject to him did not dare, however, to covet so much;
but seeing their own natural powers, they wished to rest
under his shadow, so that they no longer would serve, but
enjoy a certain liberty under him, which they saw they could
not have under the divine dominion. The angels well

knew they were destined to participate in the blessedness of rest, and to acquire that by merits and ministry. In this therefore consisted their sin of pride, that without merits they wished to be happy, to rest without ministering, and without control to pursue their own will; and this is to be proud, though not so great a sin as to covet to rule over all and be subject to none."

Yet this has by no means found general acceptance, though supported by such great names. The modern theologians when examining it find in it almost the same unanswerable objections that have been raised against the first opinion. They ask again, how could an angel's intelligence be so blinded as not to see that in God alone was supreme dominion, that every dominion held by creatures should be held subject to His, and that there could be no such thing as dominion absolute outside of His control.

(3) The great expounder and supporter of the last opinion is the learned and holy Jesuit theologian, Suarez. This opinion holds that Satan desired that the hypostatic union should be formed with his person, and this not taking place, he at once constituted himself Antichrist and raised his banner of revolt. Suarez says, when giving his adhesion to this opinion: "This is exceedingly probable; and among all the opinions put forward as to the object of Lucifer's pride, there is no one so consonant to the opinions of the Fathers, the words of the Holy Scriptures, to conjecture or to the conveniences of the subject".

No one could more fittingly use those words, "I will be like to the Highest, and raise my throne above the stars," than Christ. For a moment let us suppose Lucifer revolving

in his mind the thought of an hypostatic union and fancying
that it had actually taken place—what words could more
fittingly express his future dignity than those : " I will be
like to the Highest, and raise my throne above the stars ".
Again, since it was fitting that the hypostatic union was at
all to take place, who among creatures was it natural should
be selected but him who had come forth the highest and
most glorious of all from the hands of God ? So Satan might
argue, and there is no doubt but he knew that the most
glorious creature—the most glorious created thing—should
alone be selected for the subject of the hypostatic union,
such as in reality the soul and body of our Blessed Lord
were. And no doubt also he knew of the Incarnation ; for,
according to all theologians and Fathers (St. Basil, St.
Cyprian, St. Augustine, St. Anselm, St. Bernard, St. Chry-
sologus, St. Thomas), he knew that man was to be created,
and to be raised to a degree of glory equal to the angels ;
and with more reason should he know of the Incarnation.
Indeed, St. Bernard expressly says that it was from envy and
grief because of this knowledge that he fell—that he would
not bow the knee to dust and ashes, such as the pure body
of Christ was.

Again, it is certain that while the angels were in their
term of probation they knew that Christ was to be their
head. Now it is from the Divine Word united to human
nature that all their excellences of grace and nature came
(some theologians even say their confirmation or *redemption
from sin*) ; and it was a subject of deep slight to Lucifer
that he should be not alone passed over in the matter of
selection, but that he should even owe all his graces to a

union with a nature so immensely beneath his own, and
which he so thoroughly despised. Furthermore, an appeal
from Lucifer to his followers founded on such grounds
would be better calculated to lead them into revolt
than any founded on the divine attributes, such as God's
sovereignty.

In summing up, it is well to say that there is no need why
any of these opinions should be cast aside as untenable ; for
the intelligence of an angel, being so indefinitely beyond the
power of the human mind, may have all these at one and
the same time forming up its sin; and in the angelic intelligence, which, far more keenly than man's reason, sees
the connection (the immediate connection) between the
Incarnation* and the divine attributes, a sin could hardly
be committed against one without involving disobedience to
all. Undoubtedly there is none of those opinions explaining
Lucifer's " non serviam " (*I will not serve*) which does not
convey a most instructive lesson to us mortals in our term
of probation.

Father Faber, in his description of the Procession of the
Precious Blood, thus writes : " Now it has reached the edge
of that boundless upland. Now it stands revealed upon the
heights which face down upon creation. It passes from the
region of bright, bewildering mists—mists which bewilder
the more because they are so bright—and it emerges into

---

* Firmly I believe, and truly,
    God is Three and God is One ;
  And I *next* acknowledge duly
    Manhood taken by the Son.
                          —*Dream of Gerontius.*

light amidst created things ; or, rather, to speak more truly,
it comes, the procession of divine decrees, the pageant of the
Precious Blood, to that invisible, imperceptible point
in eternity when time should fittingly begin. At once a
whole universe of fairest light broke forth, as if beneath the
tread of those decrees, as if at the touch of that Precious
Blood. It was but an instantaneous flash, the first visibility
of the invisible God, and there lay outspread the broad
world of angels, throbbing with light and teeming with in-
numerous and yet colossal life. The brightness that silvered
them was the reflection of the Precious Blood. From it,
and because of it, they came. Out of it they drew their
marvellous diversity of graces. Their sanctities were but
mantles made of its royal texture. They beautified their
natures in its supernatural streams. It seemed as if here
the procession halted for a moment, or, perhaps, it was only
that the sudden flash of light looked like a momentary halt.
The new creatures of God, the first created minds, the
primal offspring of the Uncreated Mind, were bidden to fall
in and accompany the great procession. Oh, it was fearful,
that first sight outside the immense serenity of God !
Then truly, too truly, there was a halt, as if homage and
obedience were refused. There is a gleam, as of intolerable
battle, and a corruscation of archangelic weapons and
Michael's war-cry, echoing the first created cry among the
everlasting mountains. A third of that creation of purest
light has refused to adore the human body of the Incarnate
Word, and is flung speedily into the dread abyss. And the
ranks close in, and the unfallen light now beams more
resplendently with its thinned array than ever it beamed

before the fallen fell, and onward the procession moves."—
Precious Blood, p. 152.

The Holy Fathers say that, in addition to the sin of pride,
there was in Lucifer and the rebel angels the sin of envy—
envy of man's promised happiness, envy of the excellence of
God, envy of the hypostatic union with human nature. The
angels sinned, says Suarez, but it was not from doubting, dis-
believing, or denying ; they ever retained the full knowledge
of the truth, and it was because of that fearfully clear and
therefore inexcusable disobedience that their sin was so
great.

One would think that on this point the Puritan Milton
had been a Catholic theologian among the Schoolmen. In
Book V. the Archangel Raphael tells how "the Father
Infinite thus spake":

> Hear, all ye angels, progeny of light,
> Thrones, Dominations, Princedoms, Virtues, Powers,
> Hear My decree, which unrevoked shall stand.
> This day I have begot whom I declare
> My only Son ; and on this holy hill
> Him have anointed, whom ye now behold
> At My right hand ; your head I Him appoint ;
> And by Myself have sworn, to Him shall bow
> All knees and shall confess Him Lord.

> Satan—so call him now, his former name
> Is heard no more in heaven ; he, of the first,
> If not the first Archangel, great in power,
> In favour and pre-eminence, yet fraught
> With envy against the Son of God, that day
> Honoured by His great Father, and proclaimed
> Messiah King Anointed, could not bear
> Through pride that sight, and thought himself impaired.
>   his next subordinate,

Awakening, thus to him in secret spake—
.   .   Assemble thou,
Of all those myriads which we lead, the chief ;
Tell them, that by command, ere yet dim night
Her shadowy cloud withdraws, I am to haste,
And all who under me their banners wave,
Homeward, our flying march, where we possess
Our quarters in the north.
.   .   He together calls
Or several one by one, the Regent Powers
Under him Regent ; tells as he was taught
That the Most High commanding, now ere night—
Now ere dim night had disencumbered heaven,
The great hierarchial standard was to move.
.   .   All obeyed
The wonted signal and superior voice
Of their great Potentate—for great indeed
His name, and high was his degree in Heaven.
.   .   Now Satan, with his powers,
Far was advanced on winged speed ; a host
Innumerable as the stars of night,
Or stars of morning—dewdrops—which the sun
Impearl on every leaf and every flower.
.   At length into the limits of the north
They came, and Satan to his royal seat
High on a hill, far blazing, as a mount
Raised on a mount, with pyramids and towers
From diamond quarries hewn and rocks of gold.

Satan makes two speeches to his angels. The poet, with a
poet's art, puts insidious arguments into his mouth. The
first is thus set forth :

Thrones, Dominations, Princedoms, Virtues, Powers,
If those magnific titles yet remain,

.

Another now hath to Himself engrossed
All power, and us eclipsed under the name
Of King Anointed

.   to receive from us
Knee-tribute yet unpaid ! prostration vile !
Too much to one—but, double how endured,
   .   But what if better counsels might erect
Our minds, and teach us to cast off this yoke ?
Will ye submit your necks and choose to bend
The supple knee?   Ye will not, if I trust,
To know ye right, or if ye know yourselves.

One of the angels who owed him allegiance answers him. The poet sings :

Thus far his bold discourse without control
Had audience ; when among the seraphim,
Abdiel, than whom none with more zeal adored
The Deity   .   .
Stood up and, in a flame of zeal severe,
The current of his fury thus opposed.
O argument blasphemous, false and proud !
.   .
Canst thou with impious obloquy condemn
The just decree of God, pronounced and sworn,
That to His only Son, by right endued
With regal sceptre, every soul in heaven
Shall bend the knee?
Thyself, though great and glorious, dost thou count,
Or all angelic nature joined in one,
Equal to Him, Begotten Son ? by whom,
As by His word, the mighty Father made
All things, e'en thee ; and all the spirits of heaven
By Him created in their bright degrees.

Satan sneers, and adroitly introduces a new argument, boasting them to be gods.

That we were formed then say'st thou, and the work
Of secondary hands, by task preferred
From Father to His Son ?   Strange point and new !
   .   We know no time when we were not as now—
Know none before us—self-begot, self-raised

> By our own quickening power, when fatal course
> Had circled his full orb—the birth mature
> Of this our native heaven ;—ethereal sons,
> Our puissance is our own !
>   He said, and as the sound of waters deep
> Hoarse murmur echoed to his words applause.

Abdiel again answers :

> O alienate from God ! O spirit accursed,
> Forsaken of all good, I see thy fall
> Determined, and thy hapless crew involved
> .   No more be troubled how to quit the yoke
> Of God's Messiah ; those indulgent laws
> Will not be now vouchsafed ; other decrees
> Against thee are gone forth without recall.
> .   .   Soon expect to feel
> His thunder on thy head, devouring fire.
> Then who created thee, lamenting learn
> When He who can uncreate thee thou shalt know.
>   So spake the seraph Abdiel, faithful found,
>   Among the faithless, faithful only he.

41. *Question.*—Did the angels ever repent, or were all who sinned damned ?

Answer.—The angels never repented, and all who sinned were damned.

St. Peter says : " God spared not the angels who sinned, but delivered them, drawn by infernal ropes to the lower hell, unto torments " (2 *Peter* ii. 4).

St. Jude (i. 6) : " And the angels who kept not their principality He hath reserved under darkness in everlasting chains ".

No limitation, no qualification, is made in these texts of repentance or condemnation.

The Holy Fathers.—St. Damascene says : "All the angels

who consented with Lucifer with him fell and with him were damned". And again: "The fall was to the angels what death is to man".

St. Gregory Pope: "The angels through pride so fell that their fall can never be repaired, for never will a ray of pardon or a change of life come to restore them to the light of glory".

St. Augustine says: "God thus created the angels that those who wished could be for ever good; and those who were unwilling would never again be visited by the divine bounty".

St. Bonaventure says: "I assert with all the saints that the will of the demons can by no means be rectified, inasmuch as they are beyond their term of trial, and therefore of merit. Without doubt, God could restore to the demons a right mind; but on the part of the demons there is no preparedness for such; nay, rather their will to do good is entirely beyond possibility as reason teaches and the saints declare. To bring about this preparedness there should be on the part of the demons a repentance of the will and a healing grace on the part of God; and both these are wanting to the demons. And if you should ask what is the reason of this twofold defect, it is to be answered that the *defect of penitence* is the reason why *subsequent grace* is wanting; and if you still further inquire why this *defect of penitence*, I answer from a want of *preventing grace*, which is the effect of that *culpa* of the angels by which they have sickened and are so sick, that there is not an entrance for grace; but why this *culpa* is so irremediable there are different opinions. St. Thomas says that the *radical reason* is to be found in *the intrinsic nature of angels* and (in their own way) of disembodied souls; for a pure spiritual nature imports inflexibility into whatsoever its will has once fully and deliberately chosen."

Oh, how thankful man ought to be. God did not spare the angels, and He spared man.

42. *Question.*—Did Almighty God ever ask the angels to repent? Did He give them grace to repent?

Answer.—In the matter of repentance two kinds of grace must be taken into account. One is called *efficacious* grace, the other *sufficient* grace. By the former we mean such a grace infused into the soul that *infallibly* it will return to God or do what God wishes; as, for instance, if a man should shut his eyes against the sunlight, and the effulgence of the sun were so bright that he would have to open his eyes and see, such would be efficacious graces. Now that grace God Almighty is (*in justice*) bound to give to no one. He is blameless if He give a soul *sufficient* grace, so that if the soul wishes to correspond with God Almighty's designs, it has got from God *sufficient* grace to do so ; as a man that will voluntarily open his eyes in the daytime will have plenty of light and will not stumble. Now, in the first place, no theologian holds that God gave the angels *efficacious* grace to repent after their sin. God Almighty was by no means bound ; and had He done so, they had *infallibly* repented. As to the second grace, most theologians deny that God gave them even sufficient grace to repent. They argue thus : The angels had sinned in the light. They had seen at one glance all God's bounty; His justice was not hidden from them ; there was no obscurity as to the future they were called upon to choose. Their intellects being gigantic, it was with a vehement, gigantic, and lightning-like act of will they refused obedience to God, and therefore God refused them any opportunity of repentance.

Some theologians, however, led by that able Schoolman Suarez, hold the contrary opinion. They compare man with the angels. They admit that no one sin of man can equal the intensity of the sin of the angels. But they say, if one sin of man be not equal in malice to one sin of the angels, yet there are in man repeated sins—a repetition which amounts to a habit, and a habit which, by constant and demon-like commission of crime, becomes not alone a hunger and passion for sin, and an impossibility to refrain from it, but an open and professed defiance of God, and on account of which sinners are often called in the Sacred Scriptures *blind, hardened, cast-away.* Thus man all but equals the rebellious angels. Now, man is never deprived of the physical liberty and the ever-blessed sufficient grace of the bountiful God to return to Him ; though he may not return, and often will not do so. In the same way, they hold that it was most like the good and ever-merciful God—and so indeed it would appeal most to our own estimate of God—to hold that He left the angels the physical liberty of returning, gave them even a time (*moram aliqualem*) for repentance, and supplied them with sufficient grace, but that they would not.

PART IV.

PUNISHMENT.

43. *Question.*—Are all persons agreed as to the existence of hell, and what is hell ?

Answer.—It is wonderful the numerous opinions held as to what is hell, and whether there is a hell.

By the word hell Catholics mean that eternal punishment wherewith all the reprobates, whether fallen angels, or men who depart this life in the state of mortal sin, are punished. Hence the eternity of hell is its most terrible quality and its essence. Others, such as the Origenists, held that the reprobate—whether angels or man—would, after a very long lapse of time, repent and be restored to pardon and re-enter heaven. Now the Fifth and Seventh General Councils, in the years 563 and 787, condemned that doctrine as heresy. The Spiritualists of an early day held the same thing as to hell being merely temporary ; and Mahomet taught that some of his followers should go to hell, but that they would not be left there always. He taught, however, that eternal punishment awaited the rest of the world. The Socinians teach that wicked men—either after their death, or at furthest after the Day of Judgment—will be resolved into original nothingness, and in this perpetual nothingness they find the explanation of the Scriptures' eternity of hell.

The Protestants on this point have made a most singular revolution of doctrine. The first Protestants, when they separated from the Church, condemned prayers for the dead and denied the existence of purgatory. The latter Protestants deny the existence of an everlasting hell, and propose a temporary one ; in other words, a Catholic purgatory. This they look upon as more philosophical and more humane, and therefore more enlightened. The Rationalists of course deny the doctrine *in toto*, as an absurd and inhuman fable. Alas for poor human beings ! The pride

of the intellect and the passions of the flesh, and the suggestions of the serpent, all leading astray ; leading, like sea
robbers, with ominous light to death and swift destruction.

44. *Question.*—Will the angels be punished eternally, and
also all mankind dying in mortal sin ?

Answer.—Yes ; angels and all men who die in mortal
sin shall for ever be punished in hell.

The Scriptures say : " Which of you shall dwell with everlasting burning ? " (*Isa.* xxxiii. 14).

" And many of those that sleep in the dust of the earth
shall awake, some unto life everlasting, and others unto
reproach, to see it always " (*Daniel* xii. 2).

" Depart from me, ye accursed, into everlasting fire, which
was prepared for the devil and his angels   and these
shall go into everlasting punishment " (*Matt.* xxv. 41, 46).

There can be no question of the eternity of pains so
plainly mentioned in these texts.

Again, the Scriptures say in a negative manner the same
thing even more strongly.

" Their worm shall never die, and their fire shall never be
extinguished " (*Isa.* lxvi. 24).

" And the chaff he will burn with unquenchable fire "
(*Matt.* iii. 12).

" Better is it for thee to enter into life maimed, than
having two hands to go into hell, into unquenchable fire,
where their worm dieth not, and their fire is not extinguished " (*Mark* ix. 42).

It is furthermore proved from the unchangeableness of
the position of the damned.

"And the tree, if it fall to the north or the south, wheresover it falls, there it shall lie" (*Eccl.* xi. 3).

St. Luke tells us the answer of Abraham to the rich man buried in hell : "And besides all this between us and you, there is fixed a great chaos, so that they who would pass from hence to you cannot, nor from thence come thither" (xvi. 26).

From these texts it is apparent that after this life there is no opportunity of doing penance, there is not offered any hope of pardon, but that the state of the damned is unchangeable, and hence their punishment continues for ever.

"If it is incomprehensible that God should have existed solitary through an eternity, is it not incomprehensible, too, that He should have ever given up that solitariness and have willed to surround Himself with creatures? Why was He not content to be as He had been? Why did He bring into existence those who could not add to His blessedness, and were not secure of their own? Why did He give them that gift which we see they possess of doing right or wrong as they please, and of working out their ruin as well as their salvation? Why did He create a world like that which is before our eyes, which at best so dimly shows forth His glory, and at worst is a scene of sin and sorrow? He might have made a far more excellent world than this—He might have excluded sin; but, oh! wonderful mystery, He has surrounded Himself with the cries of fallen souls, and has created and opened the great pit. He has willed after an eternity of peace to allow of everlasting anarchy, of pride, and blasphemy, and guilt, and hatred of Himself, and the worm that dieth not. Thus He is incomprehensible to us, mortal men."—Newman, *Sermons to Mixed Congregations.*

What the Fathers say.—It must be remembered that, as a rule, it is when a doctrine of the Church is impugned that the Fathers speak with most emphasis on the point. Now the Origenists were the first to question the doctrine of eternal pains; and even before their time we have several of the Fathers using most emphatic language in regard to it. Thus—

St. Clement (Rome): "The souls of all are immortal, even of the wicked, for whom it had been better they were not incorruptible; for, punished with everlasting punishment and unquenchable fire, and to their own loss not dying, they shall never reach an end of suffering".

St. Irenæus: "To whom the Lord hath said, Depart from me, ye accursed; they shall be damned for ever".

St. Chrysostom: "Oh, that fire of hell, whosoever it seizes on shall ever burn, never have peace, and hence that fire is called unquenchable! Sinners, too, put on immortality, not for honour, but for a perpetual viaticum of their punishment; for he who has once been cast away by God into the fire may never again expect an end of pain."

This was the firm belief of the early ages. The acts of the martyrs tell us that the frequent answer of the Christian heroes was, when pressed and threatened to sacrifice to the idols, that they could not, lest they go to endless death and everlasting fire.

Action of the Church.—In the Fifth General Council (553) Origen and Theodore of Mopsuestia were condemned by a solemn anathema, and all who supported this heresy.

Reverence for the great and venerable name of Origen, that early African Father and devoted disciple of the apostolic Clement of Alexandria, makes me say a word about his life and writings, and about this sect of the Origenists, on account of his great name and his venerable hairs being brought through their action into doubtful fame.   Origen was born in the year 185, died 253, 68 years old.   This was centuries before the unworthy sect arose that sheltered themselves under his honoured name.   This sect consisted of certain monks in Egypt and Palestine, who upheld with contumacy certain errors, such as—(1) that Jesus Christ is the Son of God only by adoption, (2) that human souls existed before their union with earthly bodies, (3) that the pains of hell are not eternal, and (4) that even the demons shall one day be liberated from hell, and restored to eternal glory; and for authority they quoted the deep philosophic writings of this great Father, dead hundreds of years before. This is no place, indeed, to try to settle a question that has been a vexed one through all the centuries of the Church— namely, whether his writings gave grounds for these heresies or not.   Tillemont, in his *Memoirs* (tom. iii., p. 464), says : " His life, his knowledge, his talents made him the wonder of the age.   Yet was he still more remarkable, because of the virulent persecution that all during life dogged his steps, either through his own fault, through his misfortune, or through the jealousy of rivals.   He was driven from his country, deposed from the dignity of the priesthood, excommunicated by his own bishop and by others, at the same time that great saints believed him right and defended his cause, and that God Himself seemed to declare in his favour, by recalling through his means certain wandering sheep and inducing others to see the truth and enter the bosom of the Church, proselytes whom the Church has ever counted as her strongest defenders and her brightest ornaments. After his death the same fate seemed to pursue him that clung to him during life. Saints are found opposed to saints on the subject. Martyrs have been among his apologists, as well as among those that bitterly condemned him. Some have eulogised him as the greatest master-mind that the Church after the days of the Apostles saw ; others have repudiated him as the father of heresies that were born after his day. This latter party receiving support from an emperor who wished to dominate over the affairs of the Church, got him struck with anathema, either by the Fifth Ecumenical Council, or by another held at the same time, and which has had on this point the support of all the Greeks."

Such the man, the depth of whose genius and the extent of whose knowledge even his very accusers are forced to admit and respect. He taught school at Alexandria, and on account of his unwearied and incessant toil in writing and teaching was called Adamant. He suffered persecution under Decius at the age of sixteen. It did not please God to then crown his young life with martyrdom after the example of St. Leonidas,* his father. He was elevated to the priesthood by the bishops of Palestine, and during his life gave heroic examples of virtue. St. Gregory Nazianzen

---

* The reader will find a comprehensive and impartial account of Origen, his life and his writings, under the heading St. Leonidas, April 17th, in Alban Butler's *Lives of the Saints ;* also November 17th, under St. Gregory Thaumaturgus.

and St. Basil made extracts from his writings, and compiled them in one work. The Benedictines issued a collection of his works in 1759. This, in four volumes, seems to have been the last edition of his writings. Among his apologists were St. Athanasius, St. Gregory Thaumaturgus, and St. Basil. In everything he wrote, Origen carefully distinguished what were the dogmas of the Church and what were matters of free discussion. In the preface to his work *On Principles*, he says : "No one can regard anything as truth which deviates from ecclesiastical and apostolic tradition " " It were well," says Ferrier, " had his partisans been as docile and as submissive to the Church as he, they would not have elevated into dogmas of faith questions which he put forward as matters of opinion, and they would thus have avoided dragging his venerable memory under condemnation and his noble life into disrepute."

This unworthy and detestable sect, after its condemnation, separated into two parties that fiercely attacked each other, and after a time dwindled away from men's sight, and, were it not for the great name of Origen, would have faded away from men's memory too.

The Seventh General Council, held in the year 787, in its first act renews the condemnation here spoken of—that, namely, against the great Origen and Theodore of Mopsuestia.

The Fourth Council of Lateran, held in the year 1215, in its first chapter thus defines : " The reprobate will, with the devil, receive perpetual pain ; the just, with Christ, unending glory ". The Council of Trent speaks of pain and eternal damnation due to mortal sin.

The Athanasian Creed declares : "Those who have done good deeds will go into life everlasting ; those who have done evil into eternal fire ".

And hence it is not lawful to pray for the damned, or to offer sacrifice for them, since they are beyond all hope ; nay, we are rather required to curse them as the enemies (everlasting enemies) of God.

Theological Reason.—This is a doctrine so terrible and so menacing that at no time could it be introduced into the Church's teaching without a loud and desperate protest being raised against it. At no time of the Church is there evidence of such a protest being raised ; therefore this doctrine must have come down from the time of the Apostles.

Even the heathen poets speak of the eternity of their blessed and of their damned. What would our own reason tell us? That if God give the good eternal rewards, there is a strong presumption that the wicked suffer eternal pains. But it is so terrible to think of unending punishment. It is terrible ; but God will send no man there without himself having chosen it.

St. Bernard says a very striking thing : "If these pains had not been for ever, the Son of God would never have died to redeem us from them ". A certain proportion exists between the infinite redemption purchased by Christ and the infinite—*i.e.*, eternal—punishment induced by sin.

45. *Question.*—Would it be against God's justice and God's hatred of sin if, in the next life, sin were not punished eternally ?

Answer.—Yes; for if, in the next life, the wicked after a longer or shorter term of punishment would be restored to blessedness and peace, then that blessedness and peace would be the reward of impiety, and God's supreme authority and His divine providence could thus be slighted with impunity. Or if, after a longer or shorter term of punishment, the wicked were to be resolved into original anihilation, then there would be no examples of his eternally rigid justice ; and His divine justice, being rigid and eternal, demands that those who despise it mortally shall, in the next life, know no pardon and no respite.

St. Thomas uses the following argument : " Mortal sin is a turning away, knowingly and willingly, from God. It would not be a mortal sin unless it were an absolute turning away, and that knowingly and willingly, in a creature who is both rational and free—an act of bitter, malicious, mortal disobedience and revolt. A free reasoning creature knows that that sin is there, that that state continues—chooses to remain in that state, chooses to die in that state ; then unquestionably if he chooses to do so, God is not to blame. If he selects eternal punishment rather than God's friendship, then it is a man's own act ; and never does God refuse to receive him into favour, provided a man wishes to be received into favour."

Let an example be taken from human legislation. Civilised society has its ordinary government. This well-regulated government makes its laws and attaches punishments. If it be proved that a man with malice aforethought transgresses against the laws, then he is, in the estimation of his fellowmen, justly punished for it, especially if the laws be just ones, and the punishment be proportionate to the crime. Now God is (1) a just law-giver, and (2) the punishments He metes are scrupulously proportionate and just. Therefore if He decree eternal punishment, and that a man chooses to transgress, a man justly suffers the penalty. Again, God's own laws demand it ! In the present order of creation, who would obey His laws if eternal punishment were taken away, seeing that while it exists so many transgress them ?

Father Faber says : " It is of faith that God's harvest of glory out of that unutterable gloom is immense ; for the lost soul is as much an unwilling worship of His justice as the converted soul is a willing worship of His love.

Neither is that horrible place without a most blessed result on the salvation of many souls through the holy and salutary fear which it breeds in them, and the *loose and low notions of God* which it corrects in the unthinking. Verily it is well for our own sakes to think sometimes of that horrid place. As truly as fair France lies across the Channel, as truly as the sun is shining on the white walls and gay bridges and bright gardens and many-storied palaces of its beautiful capital, as truly as that thousands of men and women are living real lives and fulfilling various destinies, so truly is there such a place as hell, all alive this hour with the multitudinous life of countless agonies and innumerable gradations of despair " (*All for Jesus*, p. 354).

Plato says : " The wicked, whose perverse reason has deserved the fate of the reprobate, are doomed to a life of slavery and fear, and their punishments, which shall continually harass without improving them, are useful only as witnesses of their frightful and painful eternity. I know little can be made of a man's mere statement; but having for a long time weighed this matter, I find nothing more consonant with justice, reason, and the essence of truth than the fact of eternal pain."

Voltaire : "The belief in purgatory as well as in hell is of the most ancient antiquity"

D'Alembert writes to him and says : "I think I have at last hit on the certainty of the non-existence of hell".

Voltaire replies : "You are indeed fortunate ! But I am far from being so persuaded."

46. *Question.*—What is the nature of the punishment in hell ?

Answer.—The punishment is twofold : one class of punishment is essential, such as that which necessarily pursues sin ; the other is accidental, such as the fury of the demons or the wailing of the damned. Of the first description there are two kinds—the pain of *Loss* and the pain of *Sense.*

47. *Question.*—What is meant by the pain of *Loss ?*

Answer.—By it is meant the separation of the soul evermore from God.

By mortal sin the soul voluntarily turned from God. By its final impenitence it lost the power of evermore turning to Him. In this life that appeared a little matter ; but in the next, when the soul shall have been divested of the body, then it will be filled with intelligence, and that intelligence will only make it regret. The soul of the just is filled with intelligence, and it enjoys God with the fulness of that intelligence; the soul of the reprobate is likewise filled with intelligence, but it is only to wish that it had never got it.

In *Matt.* (xxv. 41) our Blessed Lord tells what will be the sentence of the reprobate : "*Depart from Me,*" &c., meaning eternal departure, eternal separation. This separation, with its consequent remorse, is often alluded to in Scripture as "the worm that dieth not," meaning thereby the continual anguish and grief of soul that shall seize on the reprobate and never leave them, because of the loss of happiness and the beatific vision for ever. And as it is beyond the sight of man's eye, and the hearing of man's ear, and the thought of man's heart to conceive the joys that God has in store in the beatific vision for those that love Him, so is it equally beyond man's power to conceive what that pain of loss is which the reprobate feel.

Christ says, moreover, that He will call them *accursed.* Now, the curse of God alone is a withering thing. God spoke, and all things were made. God spoke, and the depths of hell sprang into existence. Nothing more effective of evil can be imagined than God's curse, and therefore is that dungeon fitly called "a place of torments". Bossuet says on this word *accursed :* "It contains within itself an imprecation against the unhappy soul, which tears out from the minutest fibre of its being all the capacity it once had to receive enjoyment from bliss, as well as the power to perform the least good action" (*Meditations on the Gospel*). This pain of loss is so great as to make the pain of sense be accounted as small in comparison. St. Chrysostom says : "To have lost so much seems to me of such great pain,

that hell with all its pains were nothing but for this loss"
(*Homily on the Ep. to the Philip.*).

48. *Question.*—Do the fallen angels possess all their
natural powers and intelligence?

Answer.—Yes; they know God, they know themselves,
they know mankind. They know all that the angels in
heaven, by their natural powers, know. But this knowledge
and all these natural powers, gigantic and superhuman as
they are, are turned into destructive engines of evil—evil
for themselves and for others.

"Proud spirits," cries Bossuet, "without losing your sublime intelligence God has turned it against your own breasts
as an instrument of punishment. Everything bright and
glorious in you is transformed into evil. Those intellects,
that shone like the stars of the morning, are become the
agents of duplicity and guile."

49. *Question.*—Can they ever have a thought of doing
good?

Answer.—They never have, and they never will. As in
heaven there is never a thought of evil, so in hell there is
never a thought of good; not that the reprobate are com-
pelled, but because being separated from God, accursed by
Him, and never more capable of returning to Him, their
thoughts are continually evil.

"The angels who remained constant," says St. Bonaventure, "were confirmed through grace, and those who fell
were henceforward abandoned by God's grace. The good
were so far confirmed by grace that they cannot sin; the

wicked through malice are rendered so obstinate that they cannot have even a good thought or a good wish, although at times what they do wish for is good : for at times they wish that to be done which God wishes—and hence what is good and just—but it is not with a good will or a good intention they desire it.

" But since," he continues, " the good cannot transgress, and the wicked cannot either wish well or do well, it may appear that they have not free-will. And St. Jerome says it is God alone on whom sin cannot fall. To which difficulty we reply, that the good have been confirmed in such grace that they cannot sin, and the wicked so hardened in malice that they cannot do good ; and yet both have free-will —because, the good, without any pressure and without any necessity, of their own accord and unconstrained, select what is good and avoid what is evil, all the time, no doubt, assisted by grace ; the wicked, on the other hand, abandoned by grace, of their own choice avoid what is good and pursue what is evil, and yet they have free-will, but so depressed and so corrupted that they cannot rise to what is good.

" Nay," he goes on, " the good have free-will much more largely since their confirmation than before. For, as Augustine lays down in his *Enchiridium*, 'they are not wanting in free-will because they do not wish evil ; for much more free is that will which is not a slave to sin. Nor, again, is that will to be blamed by which the good wish to be blessed as they are—so that they do not desire to be unhappy, but that even they cannot possibly wish it (*sed nec prorsus velle possint*).' The good angels, then, cannot possibly wish evil, or desire to be unhappy ; and this is the case, not from any

privilege of their own nature, but the effect of grace. Before
their confirmation in grace the angels could have sinned,
and some did, and became demons ; and from this Augustine, in his work against Maximinus, thus argues : ' The
nature of heavenly creatures could die, because it could sin ;
and angels have sinned and become demons, and those
that did not sin could have sinned ; but if to any creature
the privilege be granted that it cannot sin, this is not from
its own nature, but from God's grace. Hence, God alone
is the only being who, not by the grace of anyone else, but
of His nature, has not sinned, does not sin, and never shall.'
That they could have sinned was then proper to them from
their nature ; that now they cannot is not from nature, *i.e.*,
free-will, but from grace ; from which grace it arises that
that very free-will cannot be so base as to bow to sin. And
thus write Jerome and Isidore."

50. *Question.*—Do these evil acts increase and re-increase
their punishment ?

Answer.—No ; the reprobate are now past the state of
meriting or demeriting. Just as the elect in heaven do not
merit new bliss by their continual praise of God, so the
reprobate in hell do not incur new punishments.

51. *Question.*—From what, then, essentially arises the pain
of loss ?

Answer.—From the ceasing of the intercourse between
the soul and its Creator ; and because of that ceasing, every
evil, natural and supernatural, follows. This is the awful
thing about mortal sin—the absolute turning away from

God, especially when by our own power we are absolutely unable *de condigno* to return again. May God in His mercy save us from, such an evil. Prayer will incline the ear of God to us, and will urge Him to stretch forth His hand to save—that is, while we are in this life ; and He Himself has said :⁄ "Turn to Me and I will turn to you ". But once the moment of final impenitence comes on—once this life is past and eternity begins—then adieu to all that is good or enjoyable for evermore.

52. *Question.*—What is meant by the pain of *Sense ?*

Answer.—By the pain of sense, the Scriptures and tradition mean *the torment of fire.* Bellarmine, Suarez, Petavius, Peronne, and others look upon *fire* as the agent of pain in hell. It has never been denied by any person of authority, and, as Vasquez remarks, is opposed to no teaching or decree of the Church. Scripture always speaks of it as "inextinguishable fire," " eternal fire ".

Tradition teaches the same. Pope St. Gregory says : " As blessedness rejoices the elect, so is it necessary (as I believe) that from the day of death fire should burn the reprobate, and that fire I hold to be corporeal ; for, when divine truth inculcates that the rich man was punished by fire, what doctor will deny that the souls of the reprobate are held in fire ? " St. Augustine says : "Incorporeal spirits shall there be imprisoned to be tortured by corporeal fires, burnt by them in strange, ineffable, but most real ways.

That Gehenna shall be corporeal fire, and shall torture the bodies of men together with their souls ; the demons, however, only spiritually, for they have no bodies.

Yet a true fire shall it be, that of both, as divine truth proclaimeth."

The Council of Florence thus decrees: "The most holy Roman Church firmly believes, professes, and teaches that no one who does not belong to the Catholic Church [*i.e.*, either to the body or the spirit] shall enter into eternal life, but shall go into everlasting fire, which is prepared for the devil and his angels" (*ex decreto pro Jacobitis*).

Reason even seems to point out the appropriateness, that the soul that has turned from God to corporeal things should by a corporeal element be tormented.

53. *Question.*—How, then, is that material fire generated? Is it extrinsic or intrinsic to the soul?

Answer.—It is a question among theologians. St. Augustine, St. Gregory, Estius, Suarez, and others hold that the reprobate are tortured in some wonderful and ineffable ways by a fire extrinsic to them, yet indissolubly united to them, and for this a positive action on the part of God is required; just as when a soul is united to a corporeal substance that we call a body, the soul is acted on by that body in some wonderful ways, that metaphysicians even are unable to account for. Even while in this life, if a person be burnt, the soul is affected mediately, that is—through the medium of the body—by fire. Others think that fire is intrinsic to the soul, deduced and evolved from the midst of the damned person. In one who is sick with internal pains, even on this earth, a fire seems to be raging. "That torturing fire in the sick person," says Bonal, "is the consciousness of the most violent separation of the parts of a living body. Now, in the reprobate there is no divine influx, whereby those parts would be united for the good of the body; therefore," he continues, " in the bodies of the reprobate there is going on an everlasting and most violent disintegration of the parts, and hence these bodies become totally and perpetually as if on fire." This might answer with regard to bodies, but it does not seem to touch at all on the subject of souls. Typically, too, the Scripture seems to say this in Isaias (xxxiii. 11) : " Ye shall conceive heat, ye shall bring forth stubble, your breath as fire shall devour you". " A fire that is not kindled shall devour him" (*Job* xx. 26). " I will bring forth a fire from the midst of thee to devour thee" (*Ezech.* xxviii. 18).

What the great St. Thomas says is this : " In a two-fold manner natural fire is generated—in its own self, from its own natural principle, evolved as in flint or coal; and secondly, artificially, and introduced by violence, as iron heated in a furnace. But whether the fire of hell exist of its own self, or in what material it exists, if a strange one, is totally unknown to us" (*St. Th. Suppl.*, q. 97, a. 6).

54. *Question.*—Is the pain of hell the same in all?

Answer.—As regards duration it is the same in all ; as regards intensity it is unequal, because proportioned to the number and gravity of the crimes. It is equal in duration, because every soul for eternity will be an enemy of God. The inequality will be because some have transgressed more, some less.

The Scripture says: " He shall be punished for all that he did, and yet shall not be consumed; according to the multitude of his devices, so also shall he suffer" (*Job* xx. 18). St. Paul says: "Do not err. God will not be mocked—as a man sows, so shall he reap" (*Galat.* vi. 8). "As much as she hath glorified herself, and lived in delicacies; so much torment and sorrow give ye to her" (*Apoc.* xviii. 7).

55. *Question.*—Are the pains of hell immutable as to intensity?

Answer.—Some, especially of the elder theologians, taught that the pains of hell may in process of time become mitigated—that is, between the date of the particular judgment and the day of the general judgment—but that even these pains so mitigated would, after the general judgment, continue unchangeable, and therefore become everlasting.

St. Thomas says: "It can be said that even in the case of the damned mercy is not wholly unrepresented, inasmuch as they are punished less than their just due. At the end of life they come to judgment damnable and damned, they therefore receive then the final retribution of their deeds, just as the saints their reward in glory; hence neither can their punishment be diminished, as neither can the glory of the saints be increased, *at least as to its essential reward—quantum ad premium essentiale.*" Thus, according to St. Thomas, if there be a diminution, it can only be in what is accidental, not in what is essential.

Taking, however, into account the parable of the rich glutton, even that accidental diminution seems to be not very strongly supported; for if anything could be accounted an accidental diminution, surely the comfort of one drop of water might; yet that one drop was to be refused, and evi-

dently our Blessed Lord meant this for a typical case.   It
may be safely said that no theologian now holds it.   Again,
the practice of the Church is directly against it.   It neither
prays, nor will it permit prayers to be offered for the damned.

"But we have not spoken sufficiently of the vastness of
the empire of the Precious Blood.   Let us look for a
moment at its extremes.   On the one hand it includes the
first-fruits of creation, the souls of infants—those flowers
whom our Lord gathers in the pure fragrance of their first
blooming ; on the other hand, the refuse of creation—those
whom God has cast off for ever.   The latter lie in outer
darkness.   Their exile is eternal.   Yet even there we find
the energy of the Precious Blood.   Inconceivable as are the
severities of hell, they are less than rigorous justice would
exact.   They are so precisely because of the Precious
Blood.   Before the days of Peter Lombard the generality
of theologians held that, as time went on, there were some
mitigations of the fierce punishments of hell.   They sank
after a while to a lower level.   There were expiations which
were only temporal and not eternal.   There were condona-
tions within certain limits.   Peter Lombard, as St. Thomas
himself says, innovated upon this teaching, and St. Thomas
followed in his steps.   Suffice it to say that, if, independent
of all hell being below the rigour of justice because of the
Precious Blood, there were any such mitigations as the
elder theologians believed, they also came, without a doubt,
from the Precious Blood.   To it alone can they be due, if
they exist at all."—Faber, *Precious Blood*, p. 136.

All the opinions of theologians are summed up in these
striking words of St. Thomas : " On account of the perfect

blessedness of the Saints, there is nothing in heaven which is not a source of joy ; so, with the damned, there is nothing in hell which is not food for sorrow, nor anything pertaining to sorrow wanting, so that their misery might be complete ". " Oh, what a terrible thing it is to fall into the hands of the living God ! "

PART V.

THE HEAVENLY CHOIRS.

It is with joy that a person turns from questions of such intense pain as those regarding hell, to speak about a subject of such beauty and attraction as the nine choirs of angels in heaven. Yet in the former subject Scripture was more explicit and more plain than in the latter. The reader must, moreover, be prepared to enter into deep and mystical discussions, yet ones which are extremely lovely in their suggestiveness, when we come to analyse the first and most sublime handiwork of the Omnipotent Creator. Father Faber says : " It would be long to recount all the marvels which theology teaches of the holy angels, of the might of their power, the breadth of their intelligence, and the fervour of their love. They are our elder brothers, the earlier family of God. The various kingdoms of their hierarchies lie before us, in species inconceivably diversified. Their graces, their powers, their gifts, their operations, their work —all are different, the one class from the other. By them they are distinguished into hierarchies and those again into choirs, and the choirs into species ; and by them also they are grouped into congenial multitudes of similar beauty, power, and office " (*Blessed Sacrament*, 281).

56. *Question.*—How many choirs of angels are there ?

Answer.—There are nine choirs of angels, distributed into three hierarchies. They are the Seraphim (*Isaias* vi. 2), the Cherubim (*Gen.* iii. 24), the Thrones, Dominations, Principalities, Powers (*Coloss.* i. 6), the Virtues, Archangels, and Angels (*Eph.* i. 2).

St. Denis, the Areopagite, the Athenian disciple of St. Paul, was the first to reckon them up; and the Fathers of the Church have unanimously followed him. These choirs, he states, differ in dignity and power. Now in every well-ordered community there must be the highest grade, the middle, and the lowest; and since these differ in dignity or grades, they are divided by theologians into three orders or hierarchies.

Tradition teaches the same. St. Augustine says : "That there are Thrones, Dominations, Principalities, Powers, I firmly believe ; and that they differ one from another I hold as indubitably true ; but what these differences are, and how great, I know not ".

St. Bonaventure says : "After what has been said, it still remains to be seen what does Scripture teach concerning the orders of angels. In several places it lays down that there are nine orders of angels—namely, Angels, Archangels, Principalities, Powers, Virtues, Dominations, Thrones, Cherubim, Seraphim ; and in these orders are three triples, and in each triple three choirs, that a similitude of the Sacred Trinity would be found impressed upon them. Hence Dionysius teaches there are three orders of angels, and he places them in triples : 'Three superior,' he says, 'three inferior, and three middle : the superior, Cherubim, Seraphim, and Thrones ; the middle, Dominations, Principalities, Powers ; the inferior, Virtues, Archangels, Angels '."

In the Ecumenical Council of Lateran held under Leo X., it is laid down : " For when in the commencement God created heaven and earth—the heavens itself He established in three Principalities, which are called hierarchies, and each of these Principalities He divided into as many choirs of angels ".

Each hierarchy is ordained that it might lead the less dignified, which is next in order to it, towards God. " This," says St. Denis, " is the firmly established law of God, that the least dignified would be brought to God by means of those more highly endowed." It may come as a question to the mind of the reader, if the first in dignity lead those of the second rank or grade, and those of the middle grade the lowest, whom do the lowest lead ? The answer is, as we shall see further on—they lead man. " Thou hast made him a little lower than the angels." Thus in all its beauty is exemplified the truth of the saying—" Order is heaven's first law ".

57. *Question.*—State the division of the nine choirs into the three hierarchies or orders ?

Answer.—St. Denis thus divides them : In the highest rank, the Seraphim, Cherubim and Thrones ; in the middle, Dominations, Virtues, Powers ; in the lowest, Principalities, Archangels, Angels. Some make a change in the last.

They put Principalities in the middle grade and Virtues in the last. There seems, however, no reason, except that it is the more common tradition of the Church. The angels' country is an unknown land. " Man's eye hath not seen ; nor man's ear heard." And he that was rapt to the third heavens only tells us that he saw and heard things unlawful to recount. Yet man will question and surmise, and these curious searchings and pious surmises are not without their use.

" An order of angels is," according to St. Bonaventura, " a multitude of heavenly spirits, who, on account of certain gifts of grace, have a likeness among themselves ; as, for instance, the Seraphim, who, according to the blessed Gregory, are alike in their ardent charity ; the Cherubim in their wisdom, and so on. These names are given to them not for their sake, but for ours ; and the individual orders are called from the gifts of grace which they possess, not exclusively but in an excellent manner ; just as men, though they possess several gifts, yet have some in a very excellent manner [and by these especially are known to the generality of their fellows], so the angels, some have some in a greater, some in a lesser degree ; but in that heavenly land, where there is the plenitude of all good, all must have all the excellences in some degree. It appears on the testimony of authority that this distinction had place from the beginning, for it lays down that angels fell from every order or rank ; and from the very highest fell Lucifer, than whom none was more dignified. It must not be concluded, however, that all angels of the one rank or order are equal. Lucifer, for instance, who was in the college of the highest, was more excellent than all his own comrades ; and had he remained firm, no doubt he would have been more excellent in glory than they. It is just the same with the Saints : There is the order of the Apostles, the Martyrs, &c. ; and yet among the Apostles there is an inequality—one being chief and supreme over all. So also the Martyrs, &c."

58. *Question.*—What do the three hierarchies, with their separate orders, represent ?

Answer.—The three hierarchies represent the three grand acts of the Divinity, and each subordinate triple order represents the threefold manner of putting these acts into operation. Now the three acts typified are, according to St. Thomas : 1st, His own essential acts theologically called *actus ad intra—i.e.,* acts respecting Himself, by which, for instance, He knows and loves Himself ; 2nd, acts relating to the whole universal creation—*i.e.,* His relations to it as Creator, Preserver, Ruler, &c. ; 3rd, acts relating to individual things or beings in that universal creation. In the first order of acts we have : Paternity, Filiation, Procession —the Father, the Only-begotten Son, and the Holy Ghost. In the second we have the creation of the world, its preservation, and its ordering; creation, conservation, gubernation. In the third we have, speaking of man, the creation, the redeeming, the glorifying ; creation, regeneration, beatification. Or, again, taking the outside world, we have the animal, vegetable, and mineral world.

Father Faber says : " But the Holy Trinity is not only the most ancient, it is also the queen of mysteries. It is enthroned over all. It embraces all within itself. It lends to all their beauty, their force, their fitness, and their divinity. It is full of depths, of mysteries that we know, and mysteries that to us are unknown. Especially does it contain *twice three abysses of external operations,* into which angels and men desire to look, and yet turn giddy as they gaze ; as much because they are sweetly inebriated with the excesses of divine goodness, as because their understanding swims and at last gives way to ecstasy in the glories of the divine power. These six abysses are : Predestination, Creation, Incarnation, Justification, Transubstantiation, and Glorification. These, with the mother mystery of the Most Holy Trinity, form the various sciences which comprise that prime glory of the human mind, the marvellous edifice of Catholic theology " (*Blessed Sacrament,* p. 269).

59. *Question.*—How do the different orders represent these acts ?

Answer.—Theologians say thus : God in His relations to Himself is represented by the Seraphim, the Cherubim, and the Thrones. We come to the meaning of those words. *Seraphim* (from the Hebrew) means *burning* or *flaming,* because of their excess of the love of God, and hence are called the flaming Seraphim. These represent the love of God ; that infinite, unconquerable, undying love. And these are put in the highest place, as created representations of that wonderful attribute, the charity of God towards Himself. In their relation to the subordinate orders also, the fiery zealots are fitly placed first, for nothing so represents the power of attracting others towards God as the being on fire oneself with love of God. "I come to cast fire on the earth."

The Cherubim are placed second in that hierarchy; and the word *Cherubim* means, according to St. Denis, a profusion of wisdom or knowledge ; according to St. Augustine, the fulness of wisdom ; according to St. Chrysostom, wisdom and purity. Now wisdom and purity, both being like light, are peculiarly typical of the Son of God. " He was the true light which enlighteneth every man that cometh into this world; and we saw His glory, the glory, as it were, of the Only-begotten of the Father, full of grace and truth."

In this first hierarchy the Thrones hold third place. The word *Throne* is taken from our own use of the expression. We understand what a throne means. It is the receptacle of royalty, and is even taken for royalty itself. Thus the love of Father and Son, the royal love of both, has found a common resting-place in the Holy Spirit ; and the resting-place is equal to the occupier—the Holy Spirit is equal to the Father or to the Son.

And again, reversing the order of the Divine Persons (since the three Divine Persons are equal), the Seraphim may be taken as representative of the burning love of the Holy Ghost, that on the Day of Pentecost came down in form of tongues of fire. The Cherubim, in this arrangement, would still be typical of the Son, in whom was the plenitude of wisdom and holiness ; and the Thrones would represent the everlasting stronghold, the eternal unchangingness, the primal cause, and mighty power and sceptre of the Father. " Salvation to our God who sitteth upon the throne." In this way the Seraphim would represent the Holy Ghost, the Cherubim the Word, and the Thrones the Father. They are in the immediate presence of God—

are placed, as St. Denis puts it, "in the vestibule of the Divinity". Their one sole business is to assist before God. "They are before the throne of God, and they serve Him day and night in His temple ; and He, that sitteth on the throne, shall dwell over them." By reason of their office they are never sent as messengers to men. To them God first imparts the knowledge of things that He wishes to make known ; and through them it becomes known to the inferior ranks of angels.

Olier says : " The Seraphim proceed from God, as flames proceed from a furnace ; and their circles surround Him as with a fiery blaze. The Cherubim are the rays of the divine wisdom, and are, so to say, the eyes of God, under which He seems to regard Himself and all the external world. The Thrones are the image of His sanctity. This hierarchy expresses the three great perfections we adore in God—namely, His love, His knowledge, and His holiness. These typify also these beautiful operations of grace, whereby God draws to Himself intelligent beings : (1) Detaching them from creatures by His love; (2) enlightening them interiorly by His heavenly wisdom; and (3) making His throne in their hearts and abiding there for ever."

THE SECOND HIERARCHY.

60. *Question.*—Which are the choirs of the second hierarchy ?

Answer.—Following St. Gregory, St. Anselm, St. Bernard, we count in the second hierarchy Dominations, Principalities, Powers. It is to be remarked that the third choir of each hierarchy has a certain relationship with the first of the subsequent one. The three of the first hierarchy were typical of the essential acts of God. The three choirs of the second hierarchy represent the external acts of God, and are typical of those in their highest order, as being nearest to His essential acts.

61. *Question.*—What is the meaning of " Dominations "?

Answer.—The title " Domination " means the fact of being in possession of all authority. Now, in the external world, the first idea pertaining to God is that He is absolute Lord of the universe. He was its creator, and therefore by incontestable right its sole Lord and Master. In this way the first of the second hierarchy is typical of that first great external act of the eternal God—His attribute of sovereign dominion.

62. *Question.*—What is meant by the term " Principalities "?

Answer.—The term comes from the word " principari," to make a beginning, to be the first to lead on, to point out the way, to direct, to legislate. Now, of all things, that which comes next in God to His attribute of universal dominion, is His setting down laws to bring all things orderly and with decorum to their destined end. This is a necessary sequence of His absolute sway, and follows hot-foot upon it. He were not God if He wanted this, at least in our present idea of God. " Through Me kings reign, and the builders of the laws decree what is just." This noble attribute of the bountiful God is thus sweetly typified by the choir of angels that we call " Principalities," and set down accordingly in its

regular order.   Hence the duty of this choir of angels is to
praise God evermore for the wisdom displayed in His
ruling and legislating for the external creation.

63. *Question.*—What is meant by the term " Powers "?

Answer.—By the term " Power " is meant the attribute
both of putting laws into execution as well as of rewarding
or punishing. In the state or commonwealth we recognise the
ruler, the legislature, and the executive Power. Now, one of
God's attributes, and that most immediately connected with
His attribute of legislating, is the power by which He puts
these laws of His into execution, and rewards obedience to
them or punishes their infringement.   And this is one of
His universal external acts, and the latest and most final ;
for He shall judge not alone rational creatures, but, in a
certain sense, even irrational ones also.   This is, moreover,
His last external work.   Now, most fitly in this second hierarchy, which represents His universal external acts, is this,
the last of them, typified by the last choir in that hierarchy.
The duty, then, of this choir is to sing God's power as
manifested daily in the carrying out of His universal laws,
and in the judgment He judges on His creatures.   Their
duty also is to shadow forth this to the inferior ranks of
angels, those of the next hierarchy.   Thus these three choirs,
forming one hierarchy, shadow forth the three-fold action of
the Creator, as absolute Lord—that is, possessing domination,
as ruler (Latin *princeps*), whence Principalities, and as executive and judge having all power, whence *potestates* or powers.
The first of these Dominations, is immediately connected
with the last of the preceding—*i.e.*, the Thrones.   Now, the

last of these Powers usually has a connection in like manner with the first of the following hierarchy.

64. *Question.*—Which are the choirs of the third hierarchy?

Answer.—The remaining ones—namely, Virtues, Archangels, Angels.

65. *Question.*—What is meant by the term "Virtues," or why are those angels so called?

Answer.—By the word "Virtue" is meant innate power or efficacy. It is thus that this third hierarchy of angels represents the acts of God towards individuals. Those works of God which surpass the power of man, as miracles or inward movements of grace, we say are done by Virtue of the Most High. With a certain appropriateness, then, comes up the statement of St. Thomas, who attributes to the Virtues the motion of the heavenly bodies and their order; these being so indefinitely beyond man's power, and thus forming, moreover, a connecting link between the duties of the other heavenly choirs which have preceded, and those two that are to follow—namely, Archangels and Angels, whose special mission lies with man on earth. The Virtues then hold an intermediate station between heaven and earth. They immediately succeed the Powers who typify the majestic judicial power of God taken universally. This third hierarchy represents that power as embodied in individual acts, and to the first choir in the hierarchy is assigned the heavenly bodies of the visible creation. "Sun, stand thou still on Gideon, and thou, moon, in the valley of Azalon." The duty of the Virtues, then, is to praise God because of His ineffable condescension in regard of each heavenly body, and to reveal that condescension to the inferior ranks of angels.

66. *Question.*—What is meant by the term " Archangel," and what by " Angel " ?

Answer.—The word " Archangel " means " great " or " high angel," and the word " Angel," the generic name for those glorious inhabitants of the heavenly Jerusalem, means a " messenger ". This name is given them because of their being employed by their Most High Lord and ours to bring messages from heaven to earth, and to carry the prayers of the faithful on earth and lay them before God's throne in heaven ; and because also they are " sent " (this is a theological word) to conduct human souls to the portals of heaven. " The title ' Angel,' inasmuch as it is the name of an office, is common to all, but is appropriated to the lower order, because it is these that are generally sent " (Bonaventure). To archangels is assigned the special protection of the Church and its several subdivisions into national churches, countries, and communities. Thus again and again in the old Bible we read about the angel of the Jewish nation—" I will send my angel before thee, and he will precede thee, and prepare thy way ". And hence popes and prelates and those in authority are said to be under the guidance of archangels. In this manner the higher grade of archangels represents the higher degrees of providence shown by God towards individuals, whether these individuals be men (as a bishop, cardinal, pope), or countries, or churches.

And thus also, as men in authority on the earth come next to the celestial bodies, so the order of archangels, coming next to the virtues of heaven, follow immediately and are in due order subordinate to them. Their office is to praise Almighty God for the vouchsafing of special providences, and to reveal these to the other angels. With the angels, as being (if so it might be said) the lowest grade in heaven, lies the intercourse with human souls, and (some have thought) with the animal and material world; and their office is to praise God for His watchfulness over even the birds of the air and the lilies of the field, and to whisper thoughts of such watchfulness into the minds of reasonable creatures, and thereby lead them to praise God.

Thus all the heavenly bodies are images of the divine attributes; more closely resembling and more especially representing some, but yet beautifully shadowing forth, as far as creatures can, all the limitless perfections and the unspeakable excellencies of the inconceivably *One* God. How appropriately after this we read in Genesis (i. 26), " Let *us* make man to *our* own image and likeness ". As the triple hierarchies of angels were like to Him, to Father, Son, and Holy Ghost, so should man be like to the Triune God. "And God created man to His own image," and " dominion," and " ruling," and " power " He gave him; " increase and multiply and fill the earth, and subdue it, and be master over bird and beast ".

"It was one of the points of ancient belief that God governed the world, even the material world, through the agency of spirits, to each of whom He was pleased to depute certain offices. He made use of the good angels to maintain order in general, to watch over empires, to protect men, and bear down to them His blessings. He permitted the evil to prove men, as appears in the history of Job, and to be the executors of His justice. Everywhere Scripture recalls this wonderful ministry of the angels, and there is not an epoch of time at which such a tradition did not exist. The Gospel shows us the Saviour Himself tempted by Satan, and narrates many of the wonderful cures of possessed persons. Our Blessed Lord teaches us that little children, dearer to him than even to their own mother's bosom, have angels appointed them as their guardians (*Matt.* xxviii. 10). Such and so great is a human soul in the eyes of God! All the heavenly spirits are ministers, according to St. Paul, and God sends them to aid us in securing our salvation (*Heb.* i. 14); to defend us against him who has been a murderer from the beginning (*John* viii. 44), and who wanders about like a roaring lion, seeking to devour us (1 *Peter* v. 8). We have to struggle not alone against flesh and blood, but against principalities and powers, against those who have dominion in this world of darkness, against evil spirits scattered in the air (*Ephes.* vi. 12).

"Faithful depositaries of ancient tradition, confirmed by the teaching of Jesus Christ, the Fathers of the Church, with an unanimous voice, tell us that the providence of the Most High is extended to all things that exist, and that it makes use of the ministry of angels for the carrying out its designs. They govern the universe and preserve it. They preside over all the elements; the stars in the heaven; the productions of the earth—fire, winds, seas, rivers, lakes—as

well as over living beings. They present to God the prayers of men. Associated with the Most High in His vast administration, they contemn not any of the duties He entrusts to their charge, and each one confines himself to his own duty alone. Thus speak Justin, Athenagoras, Theodoret, Clement of Alexandria, Gregory of Nazianzen, Origen, Euzebius of Cæserea, Jerome, Augustin, Hilary, Ambrose, Chrysostom, Cyril, and the angelic Doctor Thomas."
—Bergier.

Bossuet says: "We see before all things in this divine book (the Apocalypse) the ministry of angels. We see them coming incessantly from heaven to earth and returning again. They bring down, interpret, and execute God's orders—orders for salvation as well as for punishment. That is what is meant by the saying: The angels are ministering spirits sent for the ministry of our salvation. From the very earliest ages, the ancients believed that angels interposed in all the actions of the Church. They recognise an angel who intervened in the oblation and bore it to the sublime altar of Jesus Christ—an angel whom they call the angel of prayer, and who presented before God the petitions of the faithful (Tertul., *de Orat.*). The ancients were so touched by the ministry of angels, that Origen, who ranks justly among the sublimest of theologians, publicly and directly invokes the angel of baptism, and recommends to him an old man who was going to become an infant in Jesus Christ. There can be no hesitation in looking on St. Michael as defender of the Church, as he was formerly of the Jewish people, once we read St. John (*Apoc.* xii.), which in this case is conformable to that of Daniel (x.-xiii., xxi., xxii.). Protestants, who, by a false imagination, conceive that whatever is given to the angels or the saints in the accomplishment of God's works is so much taken from God Himself, look upon St. Michael in the Apocalypse as Jesus Christ, the Prince of Angels, and apparently in Daniel the Word eternally conceived in the bosom of the Father; but have they ever had the right spirit of the Scriptures? Do they not see that Daniel speaks of *the Prince of the Greeks* and of *the Prince of the Persians*—that is to say (without any difficulty), the angels who by God's orders preside over these nations—and that St. Michael is called, in the same sense, *the Prince of the Synagogue*, or, as the Archangel Gabriel explains it to Daniel, *Michael your Prince*, and elsewhere more expressly still, *Michael a great Prince who is established for the children of your people.* When I see in the Prophets and the Apocalypse, and even in the Gospel itself, this angel of the Persians, this angel of the Greeks, this angel of the Jews, the angel of little children who advocates their cause before God against those who scandalise them, the angel of fire, of water, and even of the stars; and when I see among these one who lays on the altar the celestial incense of prayer, I recognise here a species of mediation on the part of the angels, and I see even a foundation for the mythology of the pagans, which peopled the elements with their divinities, and laid kingdoms under their special protection—for never was there a religious error that was not founded on some truth."

"The existence of good and evil spirits, who concur in carrying out the designs of God, though in an opposite and contradictory manner, and who are, as it were, the instruments of providence in the government of the universe, even in the material world; the immortality of the soul and the state of happiness hereafter—all these beliefs, as ancient as the human race, belong to the universal tradition of man."—Cicero, *de Nat. Deor.*

A writer of wonderful research (Huet) proves that belief in the existence of angels is found among all peoples and in all lands; that the Greeks received this belief from the Egyptians and Phœnicians; and that all antiquity has recognised the existence of spiritual beings inferior to God, and created to preside over the order of nature—the stars, the elements, the generation of animals. The world, according to Thales and Pythagoras, is full of these spiritual substances. They believed that the angels floated in the sky and in the air. They divided them into two classes, the good and the evil, the latter of which was subject to the former. Plato, according to Plutarch, speaks of a prince of an evil nature, who is over the spirits that *were chased by the gods and fell from heaven.* The belief in angel-guardians, or good spirits, destined to protect and watch over man from his cradle to his grave, was no less ancient nor widespread.

———

PART VI.

OUR GUARDIAN ANGELS.

67. *Question.*—Have men on this earth angels assigned to them as their guardians?

Answer.—Yes; scripture, tradition, and theological reasoning tell us so.

Our Blessed Lord says : " Their angels always see the face of the Father in heaven " (*Matt.* xviii. 10). St. Paul says : " Are they not all ministering spirits, sent to minister for them who shall receive the inheritance of salvation ? " (*Heb.* i. 14). Many understand the following from the Psalms in a secondary sense of man, primarily, of course, of Christ : " He hath given His angels watch over thee, that they guard thee in all thy ways " (*Ps.* xc. 11).

Tradition.—St. Clement of Alexandria says : " The divine virtue gives good things by the angels whether they are or are not seen ". Origen says : "Angels have the care of our souls, and to them from our infancy are we committed as to tutors and guardians ". St. Ambrose : " An angel during lifetime belongs to man, whose care it is that no harm comes to him ". St. Bernard : " These we believe to be called angels whom we suppose to be assigned to individual men ". The Church in sanctioning an office to our guardian angels on the 2nd of October at once testifies to its belief in them. Even ancient philosophers, as was shown in the commencement of this treatise, believed it.

Theological Reason.—From what we have been saying about the angels the doctrine of angel-guardians all but necessarily follows. The first choir of angels enlightens the second, the second the third, the eighth the ninth, and the ninth mankind. Then again, and if it be true (St. Peter tells us it is) that the demons have the power of tempting man, it seems but fitting that man would be excited to good by heavenly spirits.

" It is most suitable," says St. Bonaventure, " that fallen man should be entrusted to angelic care, and that angels should be deputed to guide and direct men. God's power, God's wisdom, and God's mercy demand it : His *power*, because God wishes to be honoured, not alone *in Himself*, but even *in His servants;* whence it was not sufficient that angels should serve Himself, but that they should also minister to His creatures. Again, God had as His adversaries the demon and his followers, and it was more fitting that He should overcome them by His ministers than by Himself, that thus His power might be shown, and that not without reason He might be called the Lord of Hosts. His *wisdom;* for this is the order which the divine law follows and observes in all its operations—the lowest is brought by means of intermediaries to the highest. Now, the angels, by reason of their immortal nature and their consummation in grace, hold a middle place between God and fallen man; and it was therefore fitting that God should assist and guard man by means of angelic ministry. But, sweetest of all, it became *His boundless mercy*, that hath always opened its bosom to fallen man, and never was wanting in aught that was needful to his salvation; and hence, when fallen man *was sold to do evil* (3 *Kings* xxi. 25), He offered for him the price of the blood of His Son that *he might do good;* and because he had an enemy attacking him, He gave him a minister to be his shield, that so no part of human misery might remain unsuccoured by the divine assistance and protection. On these grounds, then, it was suitable that fallen man should be afforded angelic guidance."

Even in the state of innocence, and if man had not fallen, man would still have an angel guardian; for, says the same St. Bonaventure, "man has a struggling, not against flesh and blood, but against the rulers of this world of darkness and against the spirits of evil in the high places; and this is the reason why the good angel is sent to guard us, that we might be *defended* against the violence of our oppressor, that we might be *instructed* and *enlightened* against his deceits, and that we might be *exhorted* and *incited* to do good contrary to his wiles and temptations. Now, in a state of innocence our enemy would still have been stronger, more deceitful, and more obstinate in his evil intention than we in our purpose of doing good, and would have harassed us, though not so terribly as now; and on account of this opposition of the demon, God would have given angels to defend, enlighten, and encourage us.

"Angels have not guardian spirits; for though one angel may be said to preside over another, yet one could not be strictly said to guard the other. Moreover, since their confirmation or their fall the guidance of a guardian angel was quite useless—the good do not need it, and the wicked could derive no benefit from it; and before that event there was none to attack, and no necessity, therefore, of one to defend.

"It follows very plainly, also, from this that Our Lord Jesus Christ had not a guardian angel; for, from the moment of His ineffable Conception, He was blessed and perfectly blessed, and it belongs to the blessed *to guide* rather than be *guided*. Moreover, the hypostatic union uniting His sacred soul and body to the Divinity brought His humanity at once under the immediate protection of God's unassailable power."

68. *Question.*—Is it the just only, or have sinners and even infidels guardian angels?

Answer.—It is the common belief that not only just persons have guardian angels, but even sinners and infidels. Indeed, it would appear that sinners and infidels should more certainly have them than just people, inasmuch as they stand in far greater need of them. Now, the Scripture does not seem to limit the attendance of the guardian angels to those only who are in the state of grace, neither do the Fathers, and therefore it is likely that all have ministering spirits. It is true St. Paul seems to put a qualifying clause : " sent to minister to those who shall receive the inheritance of salvation ". But this does not necessarily exclude others. It is believed that Adam and Eve had angel guardians even before their fall. Our Blessed Lady, it is believed, had an angel guardian. It is considered that those angels that sang over Bethlehem in the Christmas sky at midnight, and appeared to the sleeping shepherds, were some of the many guardian angels appointed to attend our Blessed Lord.

69. *Question.*—Is there appointed to each man individually a special guardian angel?

Answer.—That is the general Catholic belief. The Scriptures make mention of several persons who were attended by a special angel. Thus (in *Genesis* xvi. 7) the angel of the Lord speaks openly to Agar, the angel, it is believed, that evermore was with her—her guardian angel. In Genesis also there are several mentions of an angel that accompanied Jacob. In Daniel we read of the angel of the chaste Susanna, and in the Acts of the Apostles of the angel of St. Peter. More openly, however, do the Fathers speak on the matter. St. Jerome says: "Great, therefore, is the dignity of the human soul, since each has an angel assigned to it as its attendant". The Council of Florence, in its twentieth session, approves of the epistle of St. Basil, which declares the same doctrine. And lastly, much more fully is the munificence of God and His special interest in each one of us manifested by thus appointing to each of us a special angel to care and guard and inspire us.

70. *Question.*—When does this guardianship commence?

Answer.—With the first moment of life. "Each soul," says St. Anselm, "as long as it is in the flesh is in the custody of an angel." From the moment of conception, man is a wayfarer here below, as such is exposed to the assaults of the demon, long before he has attained the use of reason, or even left his mother's womb, and as such is consequently handed over to an angel's care. From the moment the soul, which is the image of the eternal God, vivifies and ennobles the body, from that moment an angel waits on that image of the everlasting God. Therefore, our Blessed Lord says : "Do not despise one of those little ones"—long before they have attained the use of reason—"for their angels always see the face of the Father in heaven". And that guardianship ceases not till death. After death, since man is no longer in a state of probation, the guardianship in the strict sense ceases, but it is piously believed that a relationship exists, especially if the soul be saved, between that soul and its attendant guardian angel for all eternity.

St. Bonaventure asks the question, whether the guardian

angel withdraws his protection on account of obstinacy in sin? and he answers it, by saying that the angel never deserts any person, no matter how obstinate in sin, so far at least as trying to withdraw him from sin ; but he will not be as pressing in urging him to good. The wicked angel, he says, never gives up tempting a man, no matter how steadfast he may be in doing good ; and since the good angel is no less ready and desirous than the wicked, it may be fairly concluded that he, on the other hand, never deserts the man who even continues obstinate in sin. The worse a man is, the more prone he is to fall into sin; but the more prone to fall into sin, the more in need of a hand to withdraw him ; and therefore the more appealing is his claim on the angel's guidance. Again, a doctor never leaves his patient while there is life, although his case be hopeless; but our spiritual guide and doctor is God's angel, and he surely is more anxious for the welfare of our soul than the physician for the health of our body; therefore, it is to be expected that he too continues with us to the end. And even when all hope is past the doctor is still consulted as to food, and medicine, and advice—what will ease the body and soothe the pain—but the case of a soul can never be so absolutely hopeless, depending as it does on the bounty of God's grace ; and it is therefore to be assumed, that no one, no matter how obstinate, will be deprived of the angel's protection while he is in this life.

71. *Question.*—Are guardian angels appointed for countries, and churches, and communities, &c. ?

Answer.—Yes. (See *Daniel*, chaps. x. and xi.) St. Denis, St. Jerome, St. Gregory, and St. Augustine understand the

Prince of the Greeks, the Persians, and the Jews there spoken of as the angel assigned to those countries.

St. Epiphanius says : " Kingdoms and nations are placed under the guardianship of angels ". St. Clement of Alexandria : " The governancy of angels is distributed among cities and peoples ".

With regard to churches, communities, persons in dignity, monasteries, it is believed that all these have a special angel. In Daniel (x. 21) St. Michael is called the Prince of the Synagogue. In the Office of St. Michael, the Church calls him the patron and guardian of the Christian world. All the great doctors of the Church—Jerome, Isidore, Hilary— favour the opinion that each church has its guardian angel ; and it is probable that communities, monasteries, parishes, sodalities, colleges, have each their guardian angel. In the case of persons holding offices of dignity, such as popes, prelates, rulers, it is even believed that they have two—one by reason of their office, and one because of their own person —inasmuch as they need a twofold wisdom and guidance.

72. *Question.*—Have immaterial things a guardian angel ?

Answer.—The common opinion says yes. In the Apocalypse (xiv. 18, xvi. 5) we read : " And another angel went out from the altar, who had power over fire. And I heard the angel of the waters saying," &c. Again (vii. 1) : " I saw four angels standing on the four corners of the earth holding the four winds ". " And I saw another angel ascending from the rising of the sun, and he cried to the four angels to whom it was given to hurt the earth and sea." St. Gregory says : " Nothing in this visible world is disposed but by the agency of invisible creatures ". St. Thomas says : " All corporeal substances are ruled by angels, and this is the belief not of Christian divines alone, but even of pagan philosophers ". It is supposed that it is not to each individual thing, but only to the different *species* of material nature that angels are assigned.

73. *Question.*—What are the duties and acts of the angel guardian ?

Answer.—So far as they relate to persons, the six follow- are the principal :—

(1) The angel guardian defends the person from evil, and obtains and promotes the good both of body and soul. This is their direct and immediate duty ; and this they perform either by removing from our way, and all unknown to us, things hurtful and injurious, or by putting into our mind the thought of going where we would avoid harm, and meet with good.

(2) They oppose the wiles of the demons, and when the temptations of the infernal spirit would be dangerous, or when his destructive wrath might be enkindled and threaten- ing, then they interfere by opposing good inspirations to the suggestions of the evil one, and by calling, as it is believed, on the aid of the choir of angels called Powers, when physical danger is threatened from hell below.

(3) They offer up to Almighty God all our prayers. In the book of Tobias we read : " I offered your prayer to the Lord " (xii. 12). In the Apocalypse it is written " There was given to the angel much incense, and the smoke of the incense ascended from the prayers of the Saints, by the

hand of the angel before God " (vii. 3). And St. Augustine says : " The angels bear our sighs and groans before Thy Throne, O Lord, that we might more surely obtain the clemency of Thy forgiveness, and may be bedewed with the benedictions of Thy grace ".

(4) Our angel guardian intercedes for us with God, as all the Fathers teach, with a personal and special interest beyond the intercession of the other angels.

(5) From time to time they are the ministers of God in inflicting on us punishments because of our sins. Punishments for sin, it is to be remarked, may be either simply and purely penal, or they may be corrective or medicinal. When simply and purely punitive, they are ordinarily inflicted by the demon as God's minister. Executioners generally are of the lowest rank, and so the fallen angels are fitly selected as the agents of God's punitive decrees. Occasionally, however, the guardian angel is the minister ; just as, on the other hand, though the ordinary agent of God's corrective punishments is the angel guardian, yet, as in the case of holy Job, the infernal spirit is the agent appointed by Almighty God.

(6) The last hours of a man, his judgment and entrance into heaven, are the moments of the great and final duties of the guardian spirit ; and if the soul be detained in purgatory, then the duty of the angel is to offer at the throne of God the charities performed on the earth for the good of that soul, and from time to time, according to God's desires, to visit and console it in its prison of fire. Our Blessed Lord (in *St. Luke* xvi. 22) says " And it happened that the beggar died, and he was taken by angels into Abraham's

bosom ". St. Ambrose says : "These holy spirits, that is, the angels of God, are the chariots of the saints " At the great accounting day they will once more come with the Son of Man in the clouds of heaven, and then they will testify before all mankind the good actions of the glorified, the evil actions of the damned, and thus will God's justice triumph when judged.

St. Bonaventure says : "The great masters were accustomed to reckon twelve effects arising from this custody, and all these they found in the Scriptures :—

"(1) To accuse of sin. 'The angel of the Lord ascended from Galgal to the place of weepers, and said : I have brought you out of the land of Egypt, *and you have not heard my voice*' (*Judges* ii. 1).

" (2) To absolve from the chains of sin. ' The angel stood, *and the chains fell from his hands*' (*Acts* xii. 12) ; that is, the angel disposes.

"(3) To remove obstacles in the way of doing good. This is signified in *Exod.* (xii. 12), where the angel *struck the first-born of Egypt.*

"(4) To drive away demons, as we read in last chapter of Tobias : *The demon he drove away from my wife Sara,* says Tobias of Raphael.

"(5) To teach. ' *Now I have come to teach you,* and that you might understand ' (*Daniel* ix. 22).

"(6) To reveal secrets. *Gen.* xviii. 17 : The three angels have spoken of the Trinity and Unity, and continue : ' *Can I conceal anything from Abraham ?*'

"(7) To console. *Tob.* v. 13 : '*Be brave in mind, for soon you will be cured by God*'.

"(8) To strengthen in the way of God. 3 *Kings* xix. 7 *'Arise and eat, for a long way is before thee'*.

"(9) To convey and bring back. *Tob.* v. 15: *'I will lead and restore him'*.

"(10) To overthrow our enemies. *Isaias* xxxvii. 36 'And the angel of the Lord going out *struck the Assyrians* in their camp'.

"(11) To mitigate temptations to concupiscence. This is typified (in *Gen.* xxxii.), where Jacob, after struggling with the angel, receives from his hands a benediction, and forthwith *the sinew of his thigh becomes withered.*

"(12) To pray for us, and to bear our prayers before God. In the last chapter of Tobias we read: *'When you were praying with tears . I was offering them. . .'* These are the effects of the angels' custody, for all of which we ought to be grateful both to God and to His holy angels."

St. Bonaventure asks two further questions : (1) Whether the angels' joy is increased when the guarded soul is saved ; and (2) whether there is grief or pain or loss when the soul is damned ? He answers : *Essentially* there can be neither increase nor diminution of their joy in God the ever-blessed; *accidentally*, however, not alone *extensive* but even *intensive*, it is probable there may be increase. There is a joy wherein consists their *substantial* reward, a joy *in some uncreated good*—that is, their joy *about God* and *in God ;* there is another joy in *a created good*, in themselves or others—that is, their *accidental* reward. Their *substantial reward* can not be increased or lessened, since they have been confirmed in glory ; but their *accidental glory or joy*, whether *extensive* (regarding many) or *intensive* (more copiously with regard to one) may be increased, it is probable; but from man's damnation the angels conceive no compassion or sorrow, nor do they incur any loss of glory.

74. *Question.*—What, on the other hand, ought to be the reciprocal actions of man towards their guardian angels?

Answer.—St. Bernard says that man ought to show to his guardian angel—

(1) Reverence for his presence. He does this by recognising the presence of the angel every place whithersoever the man goes, and by doing nothing in his presence which, were the angel visible to his mortal eye, he would not dare to do.

(2) Devotion and affection for the angel's benevolence. The angel is to be beloved, says St. Bernard, because presently he loves us more than parent or friend, and guides towards heaven with a love that is inferior only to that of Jesus Christ who died for us, or His Blessed Mother, and because hereafter in heaven we will be brethren and co-partners in the same inheritance of glory.

(3) Unbounded confidence in his protection. We can have no fear when such a guide is by. He cannot be seduced. He cannot be overcome. The young Tobias called in terror to his guide, when the huge fish with its open jaws rushed towards him. The holy guide from heaven told him at once what to do. He did it and was saved; and not only saved himself, but he saved others also.

St. Bernard sums up thus beautifully: " They are powerful, they are prudent, they are faithful. Why, then, do we fear? Only let us follow them, only let us cling to them, and we will ever remain in God's protection." All their devotion to us, and all our indebtedness to them, is sweetly told in that little hymn which we were taught when children, and which we, in our turn, ought never fail to teach to little children :—

> " Dear angel, ever at my side,
> How loving must thou be,
> To leave thy home in heaven to guide
> An erring child like me !"

We ought also to teach little children to say the prayer to our guardian angel, and often to repeat it ourselves : " O angel of God, to whose holy care I am committed by the divine clemency, enlighten, guard, guide, and govern me. Amen !" (100 days' Ind.)

75. *Question.*—Do angels grieve over the evil deeds of those they guide ?

Answer.—Strictly speaking, angels cannot grieve ; for they are always in the possession of the Beatific Vision, and no sorrow can therefore come to them. In human conversation, however, we sometimes speak of them as afflicted with sadness and full of shame. But about the good acts of those they guide there seems no reason to doubt their gratification. Our Blessed Lord says : " There is more joy in heaven over one sinner that does penance than over ninety-nine just " ; and if the angels in heaven rejoice over a poor penitent's act, much more the angel guardian of that penitent.

76. *Question.*—In respect of the irrational and material world, what are their duties ?

Answer.—To preserve them according to the intention of God in creating those things ; to see that demons do not injure them, or make use of them for wicked purposes, and finally to direct and preserve them for their destined end in creation.

77. *Question.*—What is the duty of those angels who have guardianship of the universal world ?

Answer.—Their duty is (to use a homely figure) a sort of stewardship, to see that subordinate angels carry out God's designs, and that no clash or rupture happens in the order and harmony of the world.

78. *Question.*—Can the angels be described, or can they be seen by human eyes ?

Answer.—Angels cannot be seen such as they really are by human eyes. We in this world can have no idea of substances that are without form and occupy no space. Such are the angels of God. At times, however, they have assumed corporal shape and have appeared to men, and occasionally these outward shapes testify to their innate grandeur and power. In the book of Daniel (viii. 15) we read : "And it came to pass when I, Daniel, saw the vision, and sought the meaning, that behold there stood before me the appearance of a man. And I heard the voice of a man between Ulai, and he called and said : Gabriel, make this man to understand the vision. And he came and stood near where I stood. *And when he was come, I fell on my face trembling ;* and he said to me, Understand, O son of man, for in the time of the end the vision shall be fulfilled.

And when he spoke to me I fell flat on the ground, and *he touched me*, and set me upright."

This was merely when the angel stood near, and did not make himself visible, and yet the Prophet adds: "*And I, Daniel, languished, and was sick for some days;* and when I was risen up I did the king's business, and I was astonished at the vision, and there was none that could interpret it" But in chap. x. he describes the angel as he appeared at another time: "In the third year of Cyrus, king of the Persians, a word was revealed to Daniel. In those days I, Daniel, mourned the days of three weeks. And I ate no desirable bread, and neither flesh nor wine entered my mouth, neither was I anointed with ointment till the days of three weeks were accomplished. And in the four-and-twentieth day of the first month I was by the great river which is the Tigris. And I lifted up my eyes, and I saw and I beheld a man clothed in linen." He described his several parts. He describes his loins: "His loins were girded with the finest gold" "His body was like the chrysolite; *his face as the appearance of lightning.*" It must be remembered what lightning is, and how terrific, in the Eastern countries; "and his eyes as a burning lamp". He describes his arms and feet: "His arms and all downward even to the feet like to glittering brass"; "and the voice of his word like to the voice of a multitude"—a thousand voices put in one. He describes the effect of the vision: "And I, Daniel, alone saw the vision; for the men that were with me saw it not, *but an exceeding great terror fell upon them, and they fled away and hid themselves";* although they had not seen it. He tells of its effect on himself : " And I being left alone saw this great vision, *and there remained no strength in me*, and the appearance of my countenance was changed in me, and I fainted away and retained no strength " The Prophet continues : " And I heard the voice of his words ; and *when I heard*, I lay in a consternation upon my face, and my face was close to the ground. And behold he touched me, and lifted me upon my knees, and upon the joints of my hand. And he said to me : Daniel, thou man of desires, understand the words that I speak to thee, and stand upright. And when he said this word to me I stood *trembling*. And he said to me. And when he was speaking such words to me, I cast down my countenance to the ground and held my peace. And behold, as it were the likeness of a son of man touched my lips, then I opened my mouth aad spoke, and said to him that stood before me : O my Lord, at the sight of Thee my joints are loosed, and no strength hath remained in me. And how can the servant of my Lord speak with my Lord ? for no strength remaineth in me ; moreover, my breath is stopped. Therefore, he that looked like a man touched me again and strengthened me. And he said : Fear not, O man of desires, peace be to thee, take courage and be strong. And when he spoke to me I grew strong."

Milton, with his eagle imagination, thus paints the Archangel Raphael, whom God is sending to our first parents in Paradise to warn them against the wiles of Satan :—

So spake the Eternal Father and fulfilled
All justice, nor delayed the winged saint
After his charge received ; but from among

Thousand celestial ardours, where he stood,
Veiled with his gorgeous wings ; upspringing light,
Flew through the midst of heaven . . .
. . . six wings he wore to shade
His lineaments divine. The pair that clad
Each shoulder broad came mantling o'er his breast
With regal ornament. The middle pair
Girt like a starry zone his waist and round
Skirted his loins and thighs with downy gold,
And colours dipped in heaven. The third his feet
Shadowed from either heel with feathered mail
Sky-tinctured grain.
. . Straight knew him all the bands
Of angels under watch ; and to his state,
And to his message high, in honour rise.

Him through the spicy forest onward come
Adam discerned, as in the door he sat.

Haste hither, Eve, and with thy sight behold
Eastward among those trees what glorious shape
Comes this way moving ; *seems another morn
Risen on mid-noon ;* some great behest from heaven
To us perhaps he brings, and will vouchsafe
This day to be our guest.

In the book of Tobias in the Old Testament—that book so full of human life, human interest and romance—is to be found a most singular instance of the protection which God's beautiful angels ever tender towards man. In the early annals of the Church also, in the life, for instance, of that young virgin and martyr, St. Cecilia, to whom in our devotion we dedicate the sacred music of the altar, we find an enchanting episode where the angel of God acts a prominent and even a visible part. The young virgin, trained up in the Christian religion, with all that earnestness and tender piety which we ascribe to the early ages of Christianity, had dedicated her stainless body and soul, her heart and her affections to her God. In the interior of her own house, whether at her needlework, or among her slaves, or amid her flowers, she sang her sacred hymns, often accompanying herself on the lyre ; but ever the refrain came in—whether the burden of the song was glad or sorrowful, there was ever the one refrain, that which the Church in Cecilia's sacred office sings : " Fiat Domine cor meum et corpus meum immaculatum ut non confundar ". (Grant, O Lord, that not alone my heart, but my body also be immaculate, so that I be not confounded in thy sight.) Beautiful prayer, indeed, for a virgin saint ! And she clothed herself in sackcloth and subdued her body. But her parents gave her away in marriage. Now this was not with her own will, and therefore she said to her husband : " I have a secret to tell you, Valerian. Listen ! There is a beautiful angel and he guards me, and he will permit no one to harm me. I am a Christian." And filled interiorly with wonder, Valerian said : "Show me the beautiful angel and I will be a Christian too ! " And she replied : " You cannot see him till you are first baptised." And when he still was longing, she desired him to go out on the Appian Road, and where the sepulchres of the Saints were, he should there meet a man blind and begging, and on giving the blind beggar a signal, the white-haired old man would rise and lead him to where the holy Pontiff, Urban, was hid. And he went and was baptised, and on his return he found Cecilia praying on her knees in her bed-chamber, and beside her was the beautiful angel, and a divine light filled the whole apartment. Thereupon Valerian was so struck, that he went immediately and sought out his brother, Tiburtis. Him he brought to Cecilia, and when she saw him, she cried out: "To-day I acknowledge thee my brother, because the love of God hath led thee to despise idols," and having taught him the truths of Christianity she sent him also to be baptised ; and when he returned, he too saw the face of the beautiful angel, and the divine light filling the room. Now, the two brothers were so filled with the holy spirit of God, that they went out into the public streets and openly preached the Divinity of Christ. They were immediately taken up and brought before the judge, Almachius, and confessing themselves Christians, they endured a glorious martyrdom for the sake of their Divine Lord and Master. But Almachius, being corrupt and covetous, thought to become master of the possessions of these two brothers, for they were both very rich; and having learned that Cecilia was espoused to one of them, he sent for her, and demanded an account of their treasures and belongings. But she replied that they had already been distributed among the poor. Whereupon, being incensed, he commanded her to be taken to his own house, where he ordered a furnace to be lighted, and the slaves to cast her body into the fire. For a day and a night she remained in the fire, but not a hair of her head, nor a bone of her body, nor even the hem of her dress, was touched by the flames. As with the three children in the book of Daniel, the angel walked with her through the fire. Then Almachius ordered the common executioner to come and strike off her head Three times he awkwardly struck, and then desisting, left her neck all mangled and bloody and her head hanging, and she suffering thus for three days further, and praying all the time, slept in the Lord (*Rom. Brev.*).

To sum up with regard to the choirs of angels, those of the first hierarchy—namely, Seraphim, Cherubim, and Thrones—never leave the presence of Almighty God, and are called *assistant* angels. Their duty primarily is to honour God and praise Him; their secondary duty is to make known the will of God to the angels of the subsequent ranks. The first choir in the second hierarchy—that is, the Dominations—are called *ministering* angels, because they (as it were) order and get performed the great works of the external world, but they themselves are not employed in the performance. The remaining five choirs or orders—that is, the Principalities, Powers, Virtues, Archangels, and Angels—are called *messenger* angels, because through them and by them all the external works are executed and all the guidance performed.

79. *Question.*—Of what rank was the Archangel Gabriel who was sent to our Blessed Lady?

Answer.—It is against our preconceived notions to consider the Archangel Gabriel as belonging to any of the inferior ranks of angels, both because of the dignity of our Blessed Lady, as well as of the solemn, tremendous, and absolutely unique mission on which he came. The question arises, then, Is any member of the higher choirs ever sent on a message to earth? St. Athanasius, Scotus, Molina say yes. Great names say no—St. Dionysius, St. Bonaventure, St. Thomas. Suarez, however, says that God does sometimes dispense with the laws that guide the angelic kingdom, as He does in the case of miracles on earth ; and the common belief is that Gabriel must be one of the highest of the order of Seraphim, if not the very highest, because of our Blessed Lady and the unspeakable mystery of the Incarnation.

PART VII.

FALLEN ANGELS IN RELATION TO MEN.

80. *Question.*—Is there rank, or order, or distinction among the fallen angels ?

Answer.—Yes ; Lucifer is looked upon as the head, and the rest are his subjects. " If Satan be divided against himself, how shall *his kingdom* stand ? " (*Luc.* xi. 18). " The wicked shall go into everlasting fire, which was prepared for *the devil and his angels.*" Therefore he has power over them. They selected him as their leader, and by a fit punishment God permits him, for his and their punishment, to be their leader still. It is a punishment to them, for he domineers over them and inflicts pain. It is a punishment to him, for with the bright intelligence that belongs to an angel, and of which the rebellious were not deprived, he sees what a noble thing it would be to rule over noble souls working for a noble end ; on the other hand, what a prostitution of nobility to rule over evil agents for evil purposes. Milton, indeed, describes him as taking a demon pleasure in so ruling ; but a demon pleasure brings no joy, and so the great poet (before leaving) takes care to represent the gratification as but assumed—

What though the field be lost?
All is not lost ; the unconquerable will,
And study of revenge, immortal hate,
And courage never to submit or yield—

Here we may reign secure, and, in my choice,
To reign is worth ambition, though in hell :
Better to reign in hell than serve in heaven

So spake the apostate angel, though in pain,
Vaunting aloud, but racked with deep despair.

81. *Question.*—Is there distinction among the fallen angels ?

Answer.—Yes. It is the more common opinion that angels were lost from every one of the nine orders in heaven, and that natural rank and distinction which existed among them because of superiority or inferiority of endowments and gifts was never obliterated. St. Paul seems to point out this when he divides the demons into their several classes—Angels, Principalities, Powers, Virtues, and rulers of the kingdom of darkness. St. Thomas signifies the same, when he says that some command others, and that inferiors are subject to superiors. For the same reason that God permits the empire rule in the hands of Lucifer, we can understand that he would permit a subordinate rule in his lieutenants, that so those who were seduced should be punished by their seducers, and the seducers in turn punished by the seduced. Even such a nemesis is found in human life.

St. Bonaventure says that "after the fall, there still remained among the demons a distinction of rank, but that distinction is imperfect and perverse. It is *imperfect*, on account of the want of grace which would perfect the capability of their nature, and *perverse*, because of sin, which, though it does not substantially corrupt their natural powers, yet besmears and deranges them.

" Prelacy also there is, and will be, among the demons, until their state of *ministering* or *being sent* shall have passed away, and this for a twofold reason. First, *the children of darkness* always make attempts, no matter how false and 'imperfect, to imitate *the children of light*. These they see performing their functions according to the commands of higher and wiser spirits, and so they too in their evil ways. Secondly, they have a struggling against the human race, and their kingdom and their army, if it be without a head and divided against itself, cannot stand ; and as men fighting in battle, no matter how vainglorious or brave they individually be, yet, for hatred of the enemy and for the common goodwill, willingly subject themselves to the command of one man, their leader ; so too might it be fairly assumed in the case of the demons. And further, if it be asked, by what has this prelacy come to be ? I answer, it is not by election, nor mastery, but (as I believe) by nature and divine appointment. By their condition, there is a ministry implanted in them, in some greater, in some less ; and God ordained that the less wise and less powerful should be subject to the stronger and more cunning. And Hugo says, what they have received from the condition of their nature, that they continue to perform, so that they command one another now just as they would have done if they had continued firm."

82. *Question.*—What have the fallen angels to do with man?

Answer.—To tempt him to rebel against God as they themselves rebelled. Our first parents were so tempted. Christ says of the devil that "he was a murderer from the beginning" (*Joan.* viii. 44). St. Peter says: "Your adversary, the devil, goes about like a roaring lion, seeking whom he may devour" (1 *Peter* v. 8). St. Paul says: "For our wrestling is not against flesh and blood, but against principalities and powers, against the rulers of the world of this darkness, against the spirits of wickedness in the high places" (*Eph.* vi. 12).

Tradition.—St. Cyril says: "Truly the demon is man's enemy". St. Ambrose says: "In a thousand ways, and by a thousand wiles, the devil endeavours to overthrow man, and is much more enraged by the steadfastness of those who resist than overjoyed by the conquest of those who fall". St. Irenæus: "The devil is never at rest, nor will he leave whole nations alone, any way provided he can seduce men and lead them to transgress the commands of Almighty God".

The devil thus attacks man for many reasons from the perversity of his nature. Good men do good things from the kindness of their nature. Now, no men were ever so disposed of their nature to be kind as angels were; when the angelic nature was then perverted, none were so disposed to desire and to effect evil. Secondly, he hates man, because of God's image—the image of Him who is the greatest object of hate to the devil—because of that ever blessed image impressed on man's soul. And lastly, because of the love of God and of Jesus Christ for man, the devil hates man with a demon hatred. "And yet," says St. Chrysostom, "it brings him no gain, but even greater torments." "Ye have been reduced," says Bossuet, "to the base and malicious occupation of being our seducers first, and then the murderers of those ye seduce. Unholy ministers of God's justice, you first experience that justice, and then you increase it by trying to drag others beneath its rigours." It must be borne in mind that when the Saints speak of increasing their pains, they do not mean that the essential pain of the demons suffer change, for that is not what we believe, but that the accidental pains which belong to their position are superadded; for as a saint in glory receives *accidental* bliss and happiness by the continuation on the earth of a charitable undertaking of which he was the primary cause, so *accidental* pain is considered to be inflicted because of analogous evil deeds.

83. *Question.*—But why does God Almighty permit man to be tempted at all?

Answer.—For three reasons. (1) Because of God's own sake. Says St. Augustine: "God hath considered it more befitting His most wonder-working goodness, to draw good out of evil, than not to permit evil at all". If evil were not permitted, what means would God have, in the present order of things, to show forth the sweetness of His mercy; or would the attraction of his ever-blessed mercy be shut out from the eyes of man, and man go on through life and never be able to "taste and see how sweet the Lord is"? It is, indeed, very mysterious when we come to look at it on the part of God.

(2) On the part of man. Here it is not so mysterious. We at once recognise the justice of the Apostle's doctrine: "No one shall be crowned, but he who has legitimately striven" (2 *Tim.* ii. 5). And then again : " Blessed is the man who suffereth temptation, for when he is proved he shall receive the crown of life ". God allows temptations to us, that our bliss in heaven might be increased ; and He expressly tells us that in permitting temptation " he will not allow us to be tempted beyond our strength," and that He is ever with us : " My grace is sufficient for thee ".

(3) Because of the demon. That in being overthrown and defeated in his assaults upon men, whose natural powers as being so much inferior to the angelic he despises, he should be therefore the more humiliated and pained.

84. *Question.*—Has the demon some connection with every sin committed ?

Answer.—In one way, certainly, he has—inasmuch as he induced Adam and Eve to commit sin, and thereby brought on all the effects consequent on original sin, and which effects existing in us all are the prolific source of temptations and evil deeds. But whether he is the immediate cause, apart from that, of every sin committed, theologians do not at all agree. St. Chrysostom, St. Gregory Nazianzen, St. Thomas say, that he is not—thus holding man as the instigator himself as well as the author of sin. And indeed if man have liberty of action as he has, and if good works are imputable to him, why not evil deeds also. Yet good works are never done except by the aid of anticipating grace, and perhaps that would be a reason for holding, as St. Damascene, St. Leo, St. Denis, and St. Jerome do, that the devil's temptation always precedes a man's evil act.   This is a good deal strengthened by the answer to the following question.

85. *Question.*—Has every man a special demon to tempt him ?

Answer.—The most common opinion is, that to each man there is deputed a special demon.   The early Fathers of the Church, Tertullian, Origen, St. Gregory, all held this.   The same is taught by the greatest of modern schoolmen, Suarez. And it seems probable, for the demon attempts in everything to rival Almighty God.   Now God has given to each man a guardian angel, and the demon would therefore be supposed to assign one of the fallen angels to tempt, and therefore to oppose, contradict, and, if possible, frustrate God's designs. Therefore it is possible, nay rather probable, that that companionship commences with a man's conception, and continues to his grave, as in the case of the guardian angels.   At times that temptation may (it is believed) cease : either because the demon may hope that man may lose caution, being untempted, and that he might find it more easy to wile him after a season of peace, or that continual temptations may only lead to continual triumphs, and therefore to greater graces and higher degrees of glory on the part of the tempted ; or that God, seeing that man may yield under continual temptation, may command the wicked angel to desist ; or because of signal struggles, as in the case of the Saints, when rest may be absolutely needed.   We, however, need never fear, God is with us always.   His beautiful angel never leaves our side, and is far more watchful

and unremitting in protecting us than the evil one in
assaulting us.

86. *Question.*—How are the assaults of the demon to be
resisted ?

Answer.—The great anchorite, St. Antony, who was so
troubled by the assaults of the demons, tells us : " Believe
me," he says to his brethren, " Satan dreads pious watchings,
prayers, fasts, voluntary poverty, charity, humility, but
especially an ardent love of Jesus Christ, by the single sign
of whose cross he flies away terrified and disarmed ".

87. *Question.*—Is the power of the demon more limited
since the coming of Jesus Christ ?

Answer.—Yes. Blessed be the power of our God. In
the Apocalypse we read : " And I saw an angel coming
down from heaven, having the key of the bottomless pit,
and a great chain in his hand. And he laid hold on the
dragon, the old serpent, which is the devil and Satan, and he
bound him for a thousand years ; and he cast him into the
bottomless pit and shut him up, and set a seal upon him,
that he should no more seduce the nations till the thousand
years be finished, and after that he must be loosed a little
time " (*Apoc.* xx. 1). Now some of the Fathers understand
this passage of the power of the demons generally to tempt
man. Others think that but Lucifer himself is so bound,
and thus prevented from personally tempting man, and that
he will continue so bound till the time of Antichrist. It is,
at any rate, a fact not to be disputed, that such visible power
of the demon, as is represented by persons possessed, is not

so frequently manifested now as in former days, nor in the times after as in the times before the establishment of the Church.   Whence it may be argued that the power of the demon is much restricted.   Truly, God protects and defends those whom He loves, and will not let them be harassed by the demon ; and if at times He does give permission, He always accompanies the permission with immense graces to the person so tried.   Man may rest assured that he is safe in the keeping of his God, who will not have that the demon approach even a herd of swine without permission.

In the *Roman Breviary* under September 26, we find the following encouraging and very interesting sketch of SS. Cyprian and Justina—(this St. Cyprian must not be confounded with the great African bishop and martyr of the same name, whose feast occurs on September 16) : "Cyprian, at first a magician but afterwards a martyr, endeavoured when a young man to win by charms and potions the affections of Justina, a Christian maiden, whom he ardently desired to make his wife.   But not succeeding, he consulted the oracles, and received for reply, *that no magical art could prevail against a faithful follower of Christ.*   Cyprian was so struck with this that he flung away all his instruments of magic, destroyed all his tablets of spells and charm-words, and, grieving bitterly over his past life, became a true and earnestly devoted convert to Christianity.   When his conversion became known, he and Justina were apprehended, and professing openly the faith of Christ, they both were beaten with whips and rods, and then cast into a squalid prison.*

---

* The reader will get a most striking description of the loathsomeness of these dungeons in Cardinal Newman's famous tale *Callista.*

After some days they were brought forth, and still declaring themselves Christians, they were cast into a cauldron of boiling oil, pitch, and rezin. From this they were miraculously rescued, and at last suffered death by the sword at Nicomedia. For six days the dead bodies remained unburied, but one night some sailors stole the sacred remains, and brought them to Rome, where they were laid first outside the city in the grounds of Rufina, a gentlewoman of Rome, and afterwards in the Basilica of Constantine near the baptistry, in the city. ." (This is given at much greater length and more interesting detail in Alban Butler's *Lives of the Saints.*)

THE POWER OF THE DEMONS.

Besides the internal and invisible attacks of the demon, there are times when it pleases God to permit him to attack man in outward, visible, and extraordinary ways. " It is well worthy of your consideration to know whether demons enter *substantially* into men's bodies, or whether *they are said to enter* because they exercise their malice in harassing and oppressing human souls, and trying to draw them into sin by God's permission " (St. Bonaventure).

88. *Question.*—Is there such a thing as possession by the devil ?

Answer.—Yes. By " possession " is meant that power of the demon over the body of a person, by which he harasses it in various ways, sometimes without ceasing, sometimes at intervals. *Obsession* is different from *possession.* It is called *obsession* when the demon seems to act from outside the

person, *possession* when from within.   On this account
" possessed persons " are technically called *energumens, i.e.,*
afflicted or harassed internally.

St. Bonaventure says : " By the permission of God,
demons may enter human bodies, and worry and annoy
them.   The holy text, as also Augustine in his work on
Divination, declare that demons, by their subtle and
spiritual nature, can enter bodies, and without any obstacle
or impediment subsist in them ; and by their *power* as angels
they can disturb and harass them.   God permits this, either
for His own glory, or for punishment, or the correction of
the sinner, or for our instruction ; but from which one
of these causes definitely no one may guess, as " God's ways
are hidden ways ".

89. *Question.*—Have persons been possessed by the devil ?
Answer.—Yes.   In the first book of Kings (xvi. 13) we
read : " And Samuel anointed David in the midst of his
brethren.   And the spirit of the Lord came upon David
from that day forward.   But the spirit of the Lord *departed*
from Saul, and an evil spirit from the Lord troubled him.
And the servants of Saul said to him : Behold, now, an evil
spirit from God troubleth thee.   Let our lord give orders,
and thy servants who are before thee will seek out a man
skilful in playing on the harp, that when the evil spirit of
the Lord is upon thee he may play with his hand, and thou
mayst bear it more easily.   So whensoever the evil
spirit from the Lord was upon Saul, David took his harp,
and Saul was refreshed, for the evil spirit departed from
him."

And the Bible describes how Saul acted when the evil spirit came upon him. "And the evil spirit from God came upon Saul, and he prophesied [*i.e.*, acted like a prophet, but in a mad manner] in the midst of his house. And David played with his hand as at other times. And Saul held a spear in his hand, and threw it, thinking to nail David to the wall. David stept aside out of his presence twice. And Saul feared David, because the Lord was with him, and was departed from himself" (1 *Kings* xviii. 10).

What rage the devil must have infused into the man that would fling a dangerous weapon at another, such as Saul did! It tells of another attack: "And the evil spirit from the Lord came upon Saul, and he sat in his house, and held a spear in his hand; and David played with his hand. And Saul endeavoured to nail David to the wall with his spear. And David slipped away out of the presence of Saul; and the spear missed him, and was fastened in the wall, and David fled and escaped that night" (1 *Kings* xix. 9).

In that singularly interesting book of the Old Testament, the book of Tobias, and in its third chapter, we read that when poor old Tobias was blind, and had been upbraided by his wife, he sighed and began to pray with tears, "That the Lord would do with him according to His will, and that He would command his spirit to be received in peace, for that it was better for him to die than to live". It continues: "Now, it happened on that same day that Sara, daughter of Raguel, received a reproach from one of her father's servant maids, because she had been given to seven husbands, and a devil named Asmodeus had killed them.

So when she reproved the maid for her fault, she answered
her saying: May we never see son or daughter of thine
upon the earth, thou murderer of thy husbands.   At
these words she went into an upper chamber of her house,
and for three days and three nights did neither eat nor
drink, but continuing in prayer with tears, besought God
that he would deliver her from this reproach.   At that
time the prayers of them both [the elder Tobias and Sara]
were heard in the sight of the glory of the Most High God,
and the holy angel of the Lord, Raphael, was *sent to heal
them both.*"   In the fifth, sixth, seventh, and eleventh
chapters the way in which they were cured is told with
every detail.

We turn to the New Testament, to the evangelist St.
Mark (chap. v. 1): "And they came over the straits of the
sea into the country of the Gerasens.   And as He went
out of the ship, immediately there met him out of the
monuments a man with an unclean spirit, *who had his dwelling in the tombs,** and no man could bind him, *not even
with chains.*   For having often been bound with fetters and
chains, *he had burst the chains and broken the fetters in pieces,*
and no man could tame him.   And he was always day and
night in the monuments and on the mountains, crying and
cutting himself with stones.   And seeing Jesus afar off, he
ran and adored Him, and crying with a loud voice, he said:
What have I to do with Thee, Jesus, Son of the Most High
God?   I adjure Thee by God that Thou torment me not.
For He said unto him: Go out of the man, thou unclean
spirit.   And He asked him, What is thy name?   And he

* They were caves rather than what we would understand by tombs.

saith to Him, My name is Legion, for we are many. And he besought Him much that He would not drive him away out of the country. And there was then near the mountain a great herd of swine feeding. And the spirits besought Him saying, Send us into the swine, that we may enter into them. And Jesus immediately gave them leave. And the unclean spirits going out, entered into the swine; *and the herd with great violence was carried into the sea,* being about 2000, and were stifled in the sea."

In the same Gospel (ix. 16) we have another instance, described, too, with detail, of a person possessed. " And one of the multitude answering, said : Master, I have brought my son to Thee having a dumb spirit, who, wheresoever he taketh him, dasheth him, and he foameth and gnasheth with the teeth, and pineth away.   . And when He had seen him, immediately *the spirit troubled him,* and being thrown down upon the ground, he rolled about foaming. And He asked his father, How long hath this happened to him ? But he said, From his infancy; *and oftentimes hath he cast him into the fire and into waters to destroy him.* But if Thou canst do anything, help us, having compassion on us.   .   And when Jesus saw the multitude running together [likely, clustered together through fear], He threatened the unclean spirit, saying to him Deaf and dumb spirit, I command thee go out of him, and enter not any more into him. And crying out, *and greatly tearing him,* he went out of him, and he became as dead; so that many said, he is dead. But Jesus taking him by the hand, lifted him up, and he arose."

In the lives of the Saints, throughout the history of the

Church, are to be found numerous instances of possession or obsession, and one will scarcely wonder, when one remembers that the demon always endeavours to thwart God's works. In the *Roman Breviary* of 26th June there is an instance :—

"John and Paul were brothers, born at Rome, and living there. They had faithfully and piously, as became good Christians, served the Princess Constantia, daughter of Constantine; and when she was dying she left them a large legacy, which they expended on the poor in food and clothing.

"Julian, the apostate, being come to the throne, invited them to be of his household, but they declared they would not serve one who had turned away from Jesus Christ. Upon this he gave them plainly to understand that, if within ten days they did not change their mind, become his adherents, and sacrifice to the gods, he would have them condemned to death.

"They knew he would do as he had said, and within that time they made all possible haste to distribute their goods, and thus assist a larger number of poor people; that so, in the first place, they might have less to bind them to earth; and, in the second, have many more to receive them into eternal tabernacles. On the tenth day, Terence, prefect of the Pretorian cohort, was sent to them. He carried with him a statue of Jupiter, and the Emperor's orders were, if they did not offer sacrifice they were to die.

"The brothers were in prayer when he arrived, and, without a moment's hesitation, answered him that they were ready to lay down their lives for that God whom they adored with their hearts and confessed with their lips.

"Terence was afraid that, if these men were publicly slain, there would be a tumult in the city, so widely were they known for their good works and so greatly beloved. He therefore got them beheaded in the interior of their own house, and then industriously spread the rumour that they were but sent into exile. Their death, however, became known, and in a way that Terence little dreamt of. A number of persons were possessed by the devil, and among the rest Terence's only son, and these never ceased crying out and publishing the fact. Terence now became greatly alarmed, and, taking his son with him, he knelt at the graves of the martyrs, whereupon the young man was immediately cured. Terence and all his household became Christians, and with his own hand he wrote the lives and acts of these holy martyrs."

The Holy Fathers everywhere speak of persons being possessed, and unanimously refer to the Church's power in casting out demons as one of the signs of its divine mission. Even the very pagans have never denied the fact of persons being possessed, and are struck dumb when asked to account for their liberation by the Church's ministers. Finally, the Church, in ordaining that the power be given to exorcists of casting out demons, openly gives expression to its belief on the matter.

"Such an influence and power of the demon is not to be wondered at, if we recollect what, and how great, is the natural power of an angel (fallen or unfallen) to remove immense bodies of matter; nor, again, is it to be questioned on the part of God, who permits such attacks either as a punishment of sin or as a 'proving' and refining of virtue" (Bonal).

"Blessed is the man who suffereth temptation, because when he hath been proved, he shall receive the crown of life which God hath prepared for those who love Him" (*James* i. 12).

90. *Question.*—What is the knowledge of the demon?

Answer.—Knowledge such as an angel he was endowed with before his fall, and that we believe to be pre-eminent and extraordinary. The prophet Ezechiel (chap. xxviii.) says: "Thou, the seal of similitude, *full of wisdom*, and perfect in beauty". His knowledge far exceeds the knowledge of all rational creatures; and then he possesses a subtlety of nature, a comprehensiveness of intellect, an experience of time, and an insight into created things, that make him all but omniscient. This God has permitted that not to our own strength may we trust in our wrestling with the powers of darkness, but to Him who can give us wisdom, understanding, counsel, &c., and all other perfect gifts with the Holy Ghost from on high.

St. Dionysius, writing on the divine names, says: "We say that there were given to them (the demons) full and splendid gifts, and that these were in nowise changed".

St. Isidore (*de Summo Bono*) says: "The transgressing angels, though they lost their sanctity, never lost the fundamental inheritance of the angelic nature".

St. Bonaventure says: "There is a two-fold knowledge—knowledge of things to be known and knowledge of things to be done. The first knowledge, *although it remain substantially unaltered as to its power*, yet sometimes on account of their fall becomes somewhat darkened, especially in their judgment of contingent things ; but the second, their knowledge of what ought to be done, is wholly and absolutely destructive; and they are just as blinded in not doing right as they are obstinate in desiring it, and hence they are called *children of darkness*, and are said to be *given over to a reprobate sense.*"

"The demon, then," says an old Franciscan writer of the seventeenth century, "being endowed with such knowledge; and this knowledge embracing not alone the present and the past, but even the future, so far as the future can be foretold from deep insight into natural laws, natural causes, and effects, what wicked inventions can he not bring forth, and what malicious arts may he not be master of, and so satisfy his devilish appetite to work innumerable evils? For most plainly does he know the movements of heavenly bodies, the influences of stars, the conjunctions of planets, the mixtures of elements, the virtues of minerals, the operations of metals, the power of herbs, the properties of animals, the dispositions of men, the secret and wonderful qualities of all things—their sympathies or their antipathies—as well how they are to be applied as how they are to be modified ; what seasons and times are opportune ; what may hinder, retard, or assist their natural effects ; to select the matter which may have the power of altering, of cooling or heating, of opening, shutting, dividing, emptying, destroying ; in fine, what may be injurious or advantageous to plants, animals, or man, and of bringing about

change, recovery, sickness, death, or other evil. All these
are within his power, since he knows the species and nature
of everything in the mineral, vegetable, animal, and atmo-
spheric world clearly and most intimately, as St. Augustine,
St. Bonaventure, Scotus, St. Thomas, and all theologians
unanimously hold" (Brognolo).

It is not therefore to be wondered at that a spirit so full
of knowledge and so intent on evil should work such
extraordinary things, especially when, as holy Job says
(xli.), "there is not a power on earth to be compared to
his". "The power of the demon," says St. Gregory, "is
to be accounted indefinitely beyond all things on the earth,
because, although by his own act he has fallen far below the
condition of man, yet, in its origin, the angelic nature (which
he still possesses) supereminently transcends that of the
human race." "And with that power," says St. Bernardine,
"there is united an evil will—a will so wanton and evil, that
it wishes and desires the most wicked thing it can possibly
effect; and were it not for the infinite mercy of God it would
overturn and destroy all things within its grasp or power,
such as this world with all its surroundings; for they all,
as being inferior to the angelic state, are within the scope of
his power." We can well understand, then, that in that
unhappy empire, where he reigns and has full sway, "there
is no order, but everlasting horror dwelleth".

St. Bonaventure thus describes their knowledge of the
past: "So far as their memory as a faculty of the mind is
concerned, there can be no forgetfulness; but as a recollection or a gratefulness, they have no remembrance of God's
benefits or of His desire to have them blessed. In this

latter sense a shameful oblivion has come upon them, so much so that since their fall they are incapable of at all remembering good—*inhabiles fiunt ad recolenda bona.*"

91. *Question.*—Do men act wisely when they say, The devil take you?

Answer.—They act most thoughtlessly and unwisely. At that moment the devil would be only too glad to take away and destroy whatever his evil power is imprecated upon. It is only the Divine Will intervening that prevents him. St. Augustine says that the power of the devil has been checked by God because of his sin ; for as his knowledge on account of his fall is less than the knowledge of the angels who remained faithful, because these, in enjoying the Beatific Vision, see all future things by what is called their *morning knowledge*, whereas Lucifer, not enjoying the Beatific Vision, cannot therefore see the future in the same way as the angels in glory, and thus as his knowledge was limited by his fall, so too his power, so that he has not the same power as the angels in glory ; for although his power as well as his knowledge is fundamentally unchanged, yet as to liberty and execution—*i.e.*, in respect of its *accidents*—it is changed and limited. " From the beginning of this world God curbed the power of Satan, not in regard of his tempting man, but of his attacking or possessing him " (Brognolo).

" By the passion and death of Christ, the demon's power was singularly broken and restrained " (*Idem.*). St. Cyril of Alexandria says : " The demon had before that [before the coming of our Blessed Saviour] in his tyranny established a principality over all, and that domination he exercised mercilessly ; but by the merits of the death of Christ, and by His blood, that tyranny was broken, and that principality taken away, and those whom he pitilessly held in his grasp and power were, by the mighty conqueror of death and hell, gloriously released "

St. Hilarion, the monk, says : " By the death of Christ, the power of the demon was placed beneath our feet, and he became our slave, who, since the fall of our first parents, had lorded it wantonly over the human race ". And he continues : " Who then shall not rejoice when he reads, Now shall *the prince of this world* be cast out !—who not give thanks day and night to his glorious liberator ?" No longer can he wage civil war against the creatures of God. He is cast out. From outside he still tempts and persecutes and wages war, but foreign enemies are more easily vanquished than domestic ones.

Maldonatus on the text, " As if He should say, now shall the prince of this world be cast down from his throne and thrust out from his citadel," says, he is said to be cast out, not that he is not still in the world and possesses power over many, but that Christ so cast him out that if men wish he is fully at their mercy, and unless they bow their heads he has no power over them. In the same way it is stated in the Apocalypse (chap. xii.), he is cast from heaven to earth—heaven here being used of the Church, and earth meaning outer darkness. And again (in chap. xxx.), he is said to be bound for a thousand years, not meaning that he is cast outside the Church, or that he is absolutely bound with chains, but that his power and tyranny are so curbed and limited that if men wish he can do them no harm.

92. *Question.*—For whom does God limit his power?

Answer.—The power of the demon to work harm to body or soul is limited and shortened in favour of those whom God wishes to protect and to shelter from his attacks, either because of their faith in Jesus Christ or of their confidence in God's protection, or because of their devotion to the Blessed Mother of God, or to one's guardian angel, or to the saints.

St. Liguori says : " That as men are startled and terrified by thunder and lightning ; with such confusion and terror are the devils put to flight at the invocation of most holy Mary's venerable name ".

Lactantius says : " The demons can do no harm to those whom the high and omnipotent hand of God protects ".

Tostatus says : " It was to come to pass in time that Christ was to curb the demon's power, and therefore was it fitting that visible examples should have been given of the tyranny of the infernal spirit ".

St. Athanasius says : " So highly are they raised who have proper faith in Christ, that under their feet shall they trample that evil spirit who once dared to say, I will climb into the heavens ; over the stars shall I set my throne ; I will be like the Most High ".

St. Bernard on these words (*Ps.* xc.), " He that dwelleth in the aid of the Most High, shall abide under the protection of the God of Jacob," says : " Blessed truly is he ; for which of all the things under heaven can harm him whom the God of the heavens desires to shelter and protect ? Now under heaven are all those things which can harm, for in heaven is nothing that wishes harm—the powers of the air, the prince of this world, the flesh warring against the spirit. Well, therefore, does the Psalmist say the God of the heavens, to accentuate the fact that none of those things which are under heaven need that man fear who reposes in the protection of the Most High."

St. Hermes, the disciple of St. Paul, was often accompanied by his angel guardian in a visible form, and on one occasion the angel said to him: "Those who are full of faith in God need not fear the devil. He must depart from them, for he can find no place to enter."

In the *Life of St. Ambrose,* the learned and venerable Bishop of Milan, there is an instance very much to the point. St. Paulinus, his biographer, relates that, on account of the holy doctor's faith in God, no magician or evil spirit could harm him. After the death of the Arian Empress Justina, the magician Innocent (as he called himself) was being carried off into exile, and amid the greatest torments he declared that he was tortured by the guardian angel of St. Ambrose; for that he (Innocent) had often, at the suggestion of the Empress, who hated the Saint, tried to bring the holy man into disfavour and disrepute with the people, had made use of charms to injure him, and had even called upon the demons to kill him; that these latter gladly responded to his invocation, but that they never could get beyond the doors of the church or the episcopal palace where the holy archbishop lived.

In such ways does God curb the power of the evil one, and stretch forth His protecting hand to shield the just!

93. *Question.*—In whose regard does God permit the demon a larger exercise of power?

Answer.—"On the other hand, it may be easily gathered why the demon is often allowed the exercise of larger power, so that oftentimes men and even women are harassed by diabolical attacks, as well as injured by devilish arts, and even their lives taken away—because of a diffidence in God's power or a disloyalty to Him " (Brognolo).

Maldonatus says : " Men themselves open the door of the citadel to the demon, and by a domestic treason receive him within the gates. Therefore it is that he still reigns, and still has supremacy, but only over the children of perdition."

A very ancient writer thus puts it : " But you will ask why is it that God permits so many men to become the victims of hellish arts, and even to be murdered by demons. Why not ? As a man sows, so shall he reap. When these are sick, what doctor will they call in but the magician, the man of charms and herbs—what physician will they have but the devil ? Justly then does God permit those unhappy people to be tortured by the wonder-workers they have preferred to Him. Alas ! how rare a thing it is to find one who will put his whole trust in God ! Look at the manners of man, and everywhere you will find that God is thrust out from His own world ; and that they will go to magicians or demons more readily than they will to consult Him. And this happens age after age, and century after century—and hence the foolish fear of the supernatural that is engendered in their minds in their distrust of God " (Drexelius).

94. *Question.*—Has then the demon a larger exercise of power over the wicked than the just ?

Answer.—Broadly speaking, yes ; because of their infidelity to God.

St. Augustine, writing against the Manicheans, says : "The devil hath power against those who despise the precepts of God "—meaning large power.

Alexander Alensis, the master of the seraphic doctor, St. Bonaventure, says : " The devil has power to seduce and to destroy, unless God forbids him. With the good, however, he can exercise no power to destroy, only to tempt, and thereby to prove."

This power the demon exercises especially on his own agents—magicians, charmers, witches, &c.—whose souls are actually sold to him, and whose bodies he sometimes beats when they refuse to do his evil bidding. Even in their case, however, the power of the demon is limited. St. Augustine illustrates the demon's power by a familiar example : " The demon is like a dog that Christ has chained up : he can growl or whine, but can bite only those who come near him ".

Brognolo gives two instances, which I quote: "In the year 1648," he writes, " it happened at Venice that a boy of fourteen, named Justus, was possessed by a devil. The boy's father was called John de Taxis. I was ordered to exorcise the child, and on my asking the demon why he had entered the body of that boy, he made answer, that a magician sent him thither to take away the child from the earth. And the same answer was received on the same day from another demon who had taken possession of a girl of eighteen. But on my asking why they had not taken away the children's lives, seeing that they had already possessed them now over a twelve-month, they replied that God forbade them, and they had by no means the power to do everything they wished. And both these," continues the old Franciscan Father, "by the power of God, and by the invocation of the most holy Name of Jesus, were, at my orders, driven from these two children on the same day" (Ques. I. § 3).

95. *Question.*—Why are not all great sinners harassed by the demon ?

Answer.—It is not according to God's wish ; and secondly, the demon himself is too wise, for if he openly and violently assaulted great sinners, his dominion would be quickly curtailed ; and furthermore, he rarely attacks on this earth those whom he expects to be his for ever in the regions below, unless, of course, when ordered by God to do so.

St. Gregory says : "The demon is careless about worrying those whom he feels he shall one day have at his ease— *quos quieto jure possidere se sentit*".

The reason is plain. The one great aim of the demons is to thwart the work of God, but more particularly to thwart the work that we attribute especially to our blessed Lord— namely, the redemption and salvation of souls. The order they follow is then : try to induce men to sin, and thus to forfeit eternal salvation, but, failing in that, harass and worry them in any possible way. One great reason why, in pagan times, the demons were anxious to visibly tenant the bodies of men was that thereby their power would be more feared and extolled, and that they would be adored instead of God.

Suarez says: "The demon worries man in this way to make him impatient, to make him despair, or give utterance to blasphemy, or in some way to sin against Almighty God". "But," says Brognolo, "magicians, and charmers, and seers, and those like them who are obstinate in sin, always rushing headlong into crime, hungering and thirsting after abomination, these most grievously offend God, by their blasphemies, sacrileges, iniquities; nor even is it their own selves they bind and fetter with the chains of sin, but by their soliciting others they become the agents of Satan. Now all these the demon has no need to afflict in body, particularly as he finds them to be in mind and inclination ready and willing tools of his, and as, furthermore, he already possesses them safely and securely (*quieto jure*). This truth," continues the Father, "a certain demon, named Beelzebub, once confessed in the city of Lyons, as is related by Bartholomew Faius Regius, a councillor of the Parisian senate: 'Whilst Bursus Cilius, canon of the Cathedral Church,' he says, 'was driving the aforesaid demon out of a certain young girl named Nicola, he interrogated the demon in presence of many heretics, why he had taken possession of a child of the Church, and left so many wicked sinners undisturbed. He received this pithy but suggestive reply—Would you beat your own'?"

96. *Question.*—What are we to think about dreams?

Answer.—Dreams may, in the first place, be from God. Anyone reading the old Bible will remember that Abraham was frequently visited by God in sleep. Joseph had dreams. Pharaoh had dreams. In the New Testament the several cases of St. Joseph will be sufficient to enumerate. Dreams therefore may come from God. Generally speaking, however, they do not; and it is only in special and most notable cases that such do come from God. In the *Lives of the Saints*, we occasionally read of dreams which have a future and prophetic meaning; and these even the *Roman Breviary*, with all its staid and rigid exclusiveness, does not hesitate to put before its readers. In the main, dreams proceed from natural causes. "Although the predisposing causes of dreams may be sought for in more than one direction, they are probably in general referable to some peculiar condition of the body, and are often called into action through the agency of the external senses. Dr. Gregory relates that, having occasion to apply a bottle of hot water to his feet on going to bed, he dreamed that he was going up Mount Etna, and found the ground insufferably hot" (Chambers' *Encycl.*, art. "Dreaming").

But a person might say : "Oh, wonderful things happened to me in my sleep". Chambers, in the same article, relates some wonderful things. "Most of our readers are acquainted with the incident narrated by Coleridge of himself; that his fragment [of poetry] entitled *Kubla Khan* was composed during sleep, which had come upon him in his chair, whilst reading the following words in Purchas' *Pilgrims :* 'Here the Khan Kubla commanded a palace to be built and a stately garden thereunto, and thus ten miles of fertile ground were enclosed within a wall'."

Coleridge continued for about three hours apparently in a profound sleep, during which he had the most vivid impression that he had composed between 200 and 300 lines. " The images," he says, " rose up before him as things with a parallel production of the corresponding expressions without any sensations or consciousness of effort. On awakening he had so distinct a remembrance of the whole that he seized his pen and wrote down the lines that are still preserved. Unfortunately he was called away to attend some business, and on his return to his study he found to his intense mortification that though he still retained some vague and dim recollection of the general purport of the vision, yet with the exception of some eight or ten scattered lines and images, all the rest was passed away."

Here is another instance cited by Chambers : " Tartini is said to have composed *The Devil's Sonata* under the inspiration of a dream, in which the arch-fiend challenged him to a trial of skill. The dreamer lay entranced by the transcendent performance of his distinguished visitor, but on awakening and seizing his violin to reproduce the actual succession of notes, he produced from his general impression the celebrated composition which we have named."

Those who are readers of Irish light literature will remember that a late deceased and much-tried author introduces a personage who has composed a marvellous piece of music in dreams.

Chambers again says : " A woman aged 26, who had lost a portion of the scalp, skull, and *dura mater*, so that a portion of her brain was exposed to view, was a patient in 1821 in the hospital at Montpellier. When she was in a dreamless state or in profound sleep, her brain was comparatively motionless, and lay completely within its bony case, but when the sleep was imperfect and the mind was agitated by dreams, her brain moved, and protruded from the skull, forming what is termed *cerebral hernia*. This protrusion was greatest when the dreams, as she reported, were most vivid; and when she was perfectly awake, especially if actively engaged in conversation, it attained its highest development; nor did this protrusion occur in jerks, alternating with recession, as if caused by arterial action, but remained permanent while the conversation continued. If the data of this case are to be depended on, the appearance of the brain during profound sleep seems to indicate that during that state there is a total, or nearly a total, suspense of the mental faculties."

One other view of dreams I will consider—namely, their extraordinary and almost miraculous rapidity. Some may think that if a great deal happened in their dreams, and the time occupied by the dream was exceedingly short, it must be something unusual and even preternatural.

Chambers cites several instances. Here are two: "Dr. Carpenter mentions the case of a clergyman falling asleep in his pulpit during the singing of the psalm before the sermon, and awakening with the conviction that he must have slept at least for an hour, and that the congregation must have been waiting for him; but on referring to his Psalm-book, he was consoled by finding that his slumber had lasted not longer than during the singing of a single line".

"Sir Benjamin Brodie relates the following anecdote of the late Lord Holland: On an occasion when he was much fatigued whilst listening to a friend who was reading aloud, he fell asleep and had a dream, the particulars of which would have occupied him a quarter of an hour or longer to express in writing. After he woke, he found that he remembered the beginning of one sentence, while he actually heard the latter part of the sentence immediately following it; so that probably the whole time during which he had slept did not occupy more than a few seconds."

Young people, sick people, overworked people, are as a rule the most exposed to dreams, and to dreams of an agonising nature. If during the day anything happens which particularly engages the attention of the young, this is almost certain to recur in dreams, especially if of a dangerous or terrific nature. A boy at school hears of a ghost having been seen near his place at home. Possibly his schoolfellow has been " taking a rise out of him ". But it is no joke to the poor lad. He has forgotten it, perhaps, during the excitement of the day ; but when he puts out the light and all is dark, then it recurs to his mind, and all night he lies still in affright, or tumbling in uneasiness ; or if a step comes he wakes up with a start, horrified and terror-stricken.

Overworked, and especially over-anxious, people will be sure to dream of what is weighing on their minds. This is particularly true of literary men, or men who take part in debate, and whose minds consequently are very much strained. It is related of the great Pitt that after leaving the House of Commons, he always had a book of travels or other light literature read to him for some length of time before going to bed, and this in order to soothe the brain.

Sick people are also very liable to dreams, and dreams of a horrid nature. Everyone knows there is some mysterious connection between the human soul and the human body; but our best metaphysicians fail in explaining that connection. Sufficient for our purpose that such a connection exists. When the body is sick, the soul is affected too. When the body is sick, the humours of it are much more disarranged; and consequently when a slumber comes on the patient has horrid visions, rests uneasily, and often starts up with a feeling of choking. This is from the dreams that are begotten of the vapoury humours of the body or an overfull stomach.

In Foster's *Life of Charles Dickens* a singular dream is told. The famous author was at Genoa in the year 1844. " Let me tell you " (he wrote on the 30th September) " of a curious dream I had last Monday night. I had lain awake all night suffering from rheumatism, which knotted round my waist like a girdle of pain. At last I fell asleep and dreamed this dream. In an indistinct place, which was quite sublime in its indistinctness, I was visited by a spirit. I could not make out the face, nor do I recollect that I desired to do so. It wore a blue drapery, as a Madonna might in a picture by Raphael, and bore no resemblance to anyone I have known, except in stature. I think, but I am not sure, that I recognized the voice. Anyway I knew it was poor Mary's [his sister's] spirit. I was not at all afraid, but in a great delight, so that I wept very much, and, stretching out my arms to it, called it 'Dear'. At this I thought it recoiled, and I felt immediately that, not being of my gross nature, I ought not to have addressed it so familiarly. 'Forgive me,' I said. It was so full of compassion and sorrow for me that it cut me to the heart. [He is desired to ask a question. He does so.] I thought with myself, if I form a selfish wish, it will vanish. [He asks a question about her mother, and she replies.] ' But answer me one other question,' I said, in an agony of entreaty lest it should leave me. ' *What is the true religion ?* ' As it paused a moment without replying, ' Good God !' I said, in such an agony of haste, lest it should go away, ' you think, as I do, that the form of religion does not so greatly matter if we try to do good? Or,' I said, *observing that it still hesitated, and was moved with the greatest compassion for me,* ' perhaps the Roman Catholic is the best? Perhaps it makes one think of God oftener, and believe in Him more steadily ? ' ' For *you*,' said the spirit, speaking with such heavenly tenderness to me that I thought my heart would break—' for *you* it is the best.' Then I awoke with the tears running down my face. It was just dawn " (vol. ii., p. 123).

Dr. Murray of Maynooth College—(may his soul be with the just !)—once gave a short but most useful advice with regard to dreams : " Never think of your dreams in the morning, and never make a habit of relating or referring to them". As a rule the telling of dreams worries everybody except the narrator and some old female that has nothing else to occupy her. But has the devil the power of telling future things in dreams? To a certain extent he has. It is possible for him, for instance, to know things that are happening far away, and which, as far as we are concerned, are hidden as yet in the womb of the future. Again, he can know things much more intimately, and can therefore make a much more accurate guess at what may happen, than is possible for us. But he does not know, and cannot know, the future to a certainty. The same is to be said of gipsies and fortune-tellers. It is possible that gipsies, especially if aided by diabolic art, may tell persons things that happened in the past, and which no one but the actors themselves knew, and which therefore seem preternatural to the persons consulting them. Such an act, as well as every endeavour, by unlawful means, to read the future, is a heinous sin against God. It is taking away from God that one attribute which He has jealously reserved to Himself and refused to every creature—that, namely, of knowing the future ; and when man or woman consults fortune-tellers or the like, it is tacitly acknowledging that these are equal to God in respect of knowing the future. " Oh, such a gipsy-woman told me things that I thought the ground hardly knew ; " the insinuation of course being that if she knew the secrets of the past, why not the secrets of the future too. It is possible for a fortune-teller, by the agency of the demon, or, what is more likely, of a *confederate*, to know the locked and midnight secrets of the past ; but the secrets of the future God has reserved to Himself, and revealed to no one.

" Future events may be said to be of a three-fold nature— (1) some are of a *determined* and *infallible* character, as, for instance, the motions of the heavenly bodies; (2) others are of a *determined* but *fallible* character, as, for instance, seed cast into the ground, which generally grows up, but may not ; and (3) some are *indetermined* and *fallible*, as, for instance, things depending on our own will, and which therefore may or may not occur. In the first case even creatures may

predict with certainty; in the second, skilful persons
may predict, and that too with a degree of certainty; in
the last, no creature may predict, for no one knows except
God Almighty, or those to whom He reveals such secrets.
And the reason is, because the knowledge of creatures
pendet ex re; but, since this is an uncertain mode of knowledge, it is not possible for creatures to know or foretell
certitudinaliter. But the divine knowledge *non pendet a re
aliqua,* nay, all that He knows He knows according to *the
measure of His own truth*; and, since this truth is most
certain, He knows everything, contingent as well as necessary, in the most certain manner. Knowledge of the future
therefore belongs to God, or is from God; and hence the
declaration of all such future things is called *divination,*
because it is a divine act. But since the proud demons
desire to be honoured as God, they strive especially to show
they possess this power; and to attribute such power to
them is to attribute to them what solely and peculiarly
belongs to God, and is therefore infidelity and idolatry of
the worst type, and consequently to be avoided and ab-
horred" (St. Bonaventure).

97. *Question.*—How does the demon take possession?
Answer.—Sometimes by the order, sometimes by the
permission, of God. Suarez says: "God sometimes orders
it for the punishment of great crimes". St. Anselm says:
"God sometimes permits the demon to bring this sort of
punishment on a man for his salvation". The first then is
because of vindictive punishment pure and simple; the
second for the sake of correction.

" The demon takes occasion sometimes to enter human bodies because of their fear—fear, namely, that God cannot save them from the power of the demon ; sometimes through man's own passions, for the demon takes occasion of a man's or woman's anger or indignation to possess their bodies " (Brognolo).

According to St. Augustine, " the demon is most covetous to do harm " ; and when therefore a man does an action that displeases God, God withdraws Himself proportionately from that man, and thus leaves him more exposed to the attacks of the infernal one.

98. *Question.*—How does the demon exist in the body ?

Answer.—In a spiritual way, like the soul. There is this difference, that the soul is in every part of the body, and is there whole and entire ; whereas the demon may occupy only one member or one portion—the head, the arm, the foot, the side, the heart. He can never occupy the soul in the same way as he occupies the body. " He may be united to it by application or oppression," says St. Augustine, " but it is God alone, the soul's creator, that can substantially occupy it."

99. *Question.*—Are there any such things as ghosts ?

Answer.—We must first make up our minds as to what is meant by ghosts. By ghosts we generally mean the appearance again on this earth of persons that are dead. This appearance generally takes place at night, and, as a rule, when the person seeing it is alone. Old raths or forts, old castles, old houses, the scenes of murder or of other horrible deeds, are the places where, according to popular belief, these appearances take place. We will now proceed to examine whether it is possible for a living person to see one that is dead. No one will, for a moment, dream that it is the body that arises out of the grave. That is long since corrupted, and nothing but the archangel's trumpet shall put life into the withered flesh, and bring the dry bones together. It, therefore, is not the body that is seen; and if not the body, it can be but the soul. We will therefore discuss whether it is possible to see a soul. Is it possible to see air, to see the wind? No. Yet these are much more material substances, imperceptible and quasi-spiritual though they be, than the human soul. A man never saw his own soul; a man never saw his neighbour's soul. Why so? Because the soul is a pure spirit, and cannot be seen by corporal eyes. Can a person see the soul of one that is dead? No; no more than the soul of one that is alive. It would take a miracle from God for a person to see the soul of a person alive or dead. Now, will any sane person believe that God works a miracle every time some person takes it into a foolish imagination to think that a ghost has appeared. Preposterous! Again, the soul of the dead person is in one of three places—hell, heaven, or purgatory. If it be in hell, never fear it will not appear, even for the sake of cautioning brothers and relatives on this earth. " They have Moses and the prophets—if they will not hear these, neither will they hear one from the dead." If the soul be in heaven, it is too happily engaged blessing and adoring God, to wish to leave unless by God's express orders. If the soul be in purgatory, and granting, what some holy writers think, that a soul may spend its purgatory on this earth, it has something else to do than showing itself to benighted, half-hearted, or half-drunken travellers —not taking into account the impossibility, as before said, of our corporal eyes seeing the soul of a person alive or dead.

100. *Question.*—Is it then absolutely untrue when a person says he has seen a ghost ; or does anything preternatural appear ?

Answer.—It is possible that God may permit a soul to return from the other world, and appear to one on this earth ; but plainly this must be for some weighty and important reason. In the book of Kings it is told that the witch of Endor brought up by her incantations the ghost of the prophet Samuel to king Saul ; but commentators are divided whether this was really the soul of the prophet or merely an appearance ; the latter is the more general opinion, because if Samuel appeared in reality, the witch would then possess divine power. Our blessed Lord did undoubtedly bring back from the other world the souls of many persons. But these were miracles—miracles wrought with a divine purpose—that, namely, of proving the truth of His heavenly mission. Such also has been the case in the instances of His Saints doing the like. Now, where does such a reason exist in the thousand and one occurrences that we may hear of every day ? If an appearance really takes place, that appearance is to be *prima facie* attributed to the demon.

"The demons," says St. Bonaventure, "can produce artificial forms by their own power, but the natural living things they cannot. As man may make figures and images,

even so the demon; but it is God alone who, of His own
power, can create things that did not already exist, or form
things from things not existing.   Therefore, in the case of the
serpents, they were merely imitations, which the Egyptian
sorcerers, by the aid of the demon, were permitted to produce before Pharao, and not real creatures.

"Thus, too, angels (whether good or bad) sometimes
assume human bodies as instruments, signs, and dwelling-
places; as *instruments* or *organs*, to work with; as *signs*, to
manifest themselves; as *coverings or dwelling-places*, to converse.   These they assume as a man might his clothes;
and thus it is plain that it is not for anything to be done to
the assumed bodies themselves, but to make use of them
for *working*, for *manifesting*, for *conversing*.   While thus
assumed, the body follows the laws of spirit, rather than,
conversely, the spirit the laws of bodies, because it is by the
spirit it is formed, by it it is conserved, and by it it is ruled.
These bodies are not true bodies, nor have they complete
organisation such as human bodies have; they are merely
effigies or appearances of bodies; for if an angel would
form a human body *de novo*, there is no reason why it may
not also raise up a dead body from the grave, and that has
never been permitted to it."

St. Bonaventure asks the question, Where, and how, and
of what are these assumed bodies formed?   "On this
matter," he replies, "learned men have held different
opinions.   Some have thought that the angels assume these
bodies *ex natura elemantari*, but yet not from one thing but
from many—one, however, predominating; and hence they
look on this assumed body as a truly *mixed* body, though

no1 a truly *human* one. Others think that these assumed bodies are formed out of the air; the angels, by some process known to them, condensing it (as, for instance, water by cold is changed into ice), and thus these bodies asaume the outward shape and appearance of human bodies. There is still a third way," continues the saint, "which seems the most probable, that these bodies assumed by the angels are elementary; not that they are formed in certain proportions of the four elementary things such as organised bodies are, but that principally they are formed of air, with a certain mixture of another element; just, for instance, as the clouds, which, though they be not fully mixed, yet are formed from more than one element. It does not, then, need that an angel should search at great trouble for matter for their bodies, since the air, to a certain extent, is always a mixture of two or more elements.

"Such bodies cannot exercise the natural functions of human bodies. They do not make use of food. It is written in the twelfth chapter of Tobias : 'I seemed indeed to you to eat and drink ; but I make use of food and drink that is invisible '. An assumed body, then, has not power to convert food into itself, &c., but it sometimes exercises operations somewhat similar to the functions of the human body, though not real."

As I have already dwelt at length on this subject, I will merely quote authorities : St. Augustine, his book on *Heresy*, chap. lxviii.; *City of God*, Book X., chap. ii. ; St. Chrysostom, *Homily* 29, on St. Matthew; St. Thomas, I. Par., qu. 117 ; Sanchez, I. ; Decal., Book II.

But it will be urged that these appearances have told

persons to make restitution in their name, to get prayers said for them, or have masses offered. Even so, "great caution is to be exercised with regard to such apparitions; for without a particular grace of God, no one can safely assert which are genuine and which are not, especially as St. Paul testifies that the discretion of spirits is a gratuitous gift of God" (1 *Cor.* xiii., Brognolo). The demon may thus put on the appearance of an angel of light, in order the more surely to deceive the unwary.

The devotion to the holy souls in purgatory is a very great charity towards God, towards Jesus Christ, towards guardian angels, but especially towards our deceased relatives and friends; for that reason I wish to add one word more. I am one who will believe that the angel-guardian of a soul detained in purgatory may put it into the mind of a relative or friend on this earth to say a prayer, give a charity, offer holy communion, or procure a mass to be celebrated for the soul of the deceased. I will even believe that that intimation may come during sleep. I am anxious that the soul in purgatory should not forfeit the slightest chance of being remembered or relieved. But I very distinctly refuse to believe in any appearance whatsoever. That, so far as I can understand the case, except under most exceptional circumstances, is the work of the demon, or the product of a deranged imagination. I am totally abstracting here from such apparitions as our Blessed Lady at Lourdes or elsewhere.

101. *Question.*—What about forts, fairies, good people, &c., &c.?

Answer.—The forts we see scattered through the country, and which so enhance and beautify the scenery, were, a great many of them, the ancient dwelling-places of our forefathers. They were built in a circular form, and protected with stakes driven in the ground for shelter and defence. Some are larger than others, just as some of our dwellings to-day are larger than others, implying thereby a higher rank, a larger family, or what is commonly spoken of as a larger " following ". In some cases they were inhabited by but one family; and the cattle belonging to it, like the Arab's horse, all but slept with the family. Solitary dwellers, however, were the exceptions : many families living together was the rule. Our forefathers had not the same notions of architecture as we have. They threw up a mound of earth, palisaded it all round, made some excavations in the heap of clay, which served as the place of their cabins, and then covered them over with the green boughs of the forest. This was the origin of our forts; and if one can realise the state of society during the chieftaincies of Ireland, and the irruptions of the Danes, one will see—will readily see—how admirably adapted were those rude structures to the necessities of the times, being capable of reconstruction on the evening of the very day they were burnt and destroyed. I should be tempted to go at some length into this question, but the subject will be found fully and exhaustively treated in our Irish histories and other collateral works, especially those of Dr. Petrie, Dr. O'Donovan, Professor O'Curry, and in our own day in the works of Mr. Joyce.

In a qualified way I am glad that our forts have the reputation of being haunted, as they are thus saved from the hand of the spoiler. It would be a great drawback to the picturesqueness of the landscape, as it would be a great historical loss, if any of these our most revered, most ancient, most characteristic, and most lasting national landmarks, or their more stately brethren, the round towers, "those dials of ages," were removed. We are reminded of four different classes and periods when we look to (1) our round towers, (2) our fairy forts, (3) our ivied ecclesiastical ruins, and (4) our dismantled castles and strongholds. All these, in the popular mind, have become entwined with ghostly stories.

What then have we to say of fairies? No such things exist. Or good-people? No such things exist. Or leprechauns or phookas? Alas for fairy-tales! no such things exist! It is not told us anywhere—and if it be, it must be a very hidden place—that God made fairies, or good-people, or phookas. And if God did not make them, they could not be. God made everything in heaven and earth. To be sure, God made angels, and some of them fell, and some of these are called the powers of the air—but that is all!

102. *Question.*—What is obsession?

Answer.—We speak of obsession when the devil assumes a visible form, and from time to time attacks a person from outside the body. A most notable example of this took place in recent times in the city of Limerick, and lest, through want of thought, it might be said, "no portents now our foes amaze," I will transcribe a description of an obsession from the work of a right reverend author, lately deceased.

At page 216 Miss Tyrrell tells about her maid Emma

Crane, the obsessed girl: "She came to me only on Monday, and her melancholy look interested me in her behalf.

Tuesday, Wednesday, Thursday, yesterday, passed. Last night she was discovered lying on the floor torn and bleeding, head, face, neck, and shoulders, and for a long while after the discovery scarcely able to explain her sad fate."

Miss Tyrrell tells how it commenced: "On a calm summer evening, just the 20th of last May, she sat in an arbour which belonged to the garden of a dwelling in which she had been employed. Poor Emma had a mind to see the delicate beauties of the fresh young leaves, and her eyes wandered from her work   when her heart began to beat, and she became alarmed. She called back her thoughts, and forcing her looks on the path before her, she saw crouched, with bared teeth and blazing eye, a huge, greyish rat. She screamed, called upon God and the Virgin Mary, and fainted. The poor girl heard and felt no more till she found herself in bed, with various applications to her head and neck, and weltering in her blood."

Emma is introduced, and she herself tells the remainder of it: "In a quarter of an hour or less Emma Crane presented herself. She was an interesting young woman of one and twenty. She was deadly pale, and her neck was swathed with linens.   'All the world was flying from me,' she said, 'when they heard of it. I could get no employment, and scarcely a lodging; while every day for a week my terrible curse appeared to me and attacked me. I had only one friend, and he always trusted me, sharing with me the little he could obtain from his calling.' (This was her confessor.) 'He has been to me the angel of God—long

since, I fear, I should have died by my own hand but for
him. Oh!' cried Emma, falling on her knees, 'wherever
he is, may the light of heaven be in his heart and on his
head! What would have become of me only for him?

"'Well, sir,' continued Emma, 'I presented myself to
him time after time, all bloody and nearly mad. Oh! the
agony that came with the night-time! and the doom that
came in the shadows! I could not, dare not, lie
down! And then my blood would freeze, and the room
would rock; and while I yet looked—oh, God! oh, Virgin
Mother!—the demon stood before me on the floor, and lay
down just as I saw him the first terrible day before he flew
at my throat and tore me!'

"Emma shuddered!

"'You went to your confessor regularly?'

"'Yes! oh, yes! I should have died but for *that*. He
made me live on, "under the hand of God". He gave me
his small means, and endeavoured to obtain work for me.
But I lived in continued excitement; and my brain used to
burn, and, in fits of desperation—crazed from the memory
of the night past, and maddened by the fear of the night to
come—I have gone to drown myself. The poor
people were beginning to be frightened at my approach, and
the little children that used to play with me, and love me,
flew shrieking away when I came near. The shopkeepers
prayed I wouldn't come to their places, and the tradespeoplè
were "not home" for me. Everything and everyone became my enemy, and my heart was blackening against the
world. The world was an enemy—only *him*, and the
warm love of God came into my heart when he spoke.'

"'He relieved you from the monster?'

"'*He believed in me.* Oh, may God bless him, he did; only for that I should now be in hell; it struck him to obtain leave for me to lie on the boards in the sacristy, looking at the light that hung before Jesus. How happy I was there! For over four months I have lain on the sacristy-floor at night, and worked there during the day, and for four months my soul was in heaven.'

"'You were not allowed to stay?'

"'The parish clergyman, merciful and good, was cautious. He said: "However true she is she cannot always remain here, and whatever may be done last may as well be done first".'

"She went to London, hoping that in a strange country and across the seas she would be free from her demon tormentor.

"'For three days I made up my mind that I had left the demon beyond the sea, but last night—oh! mother of God! —having risen from my knees the creature stood there before me! The same malignant eye was on me, and the bloody teeth were bare—oh, God!' She had to return home.

"The little room was like a chapel. An altar occupied one corner, in which there was a small tabernacle. . A lamp burned before the tabernacle. Poor Emma Crane lay on a small sofa, her neck covered, and her cheeks torn, and her eyes bloodshot.

"'You have been attacked again?' asked Ailey.

"'Alas!' she cried, uncovering her neck and showing some frightful gashes—'alas! three times this day and a half.'

" ' But I thought,' Ailey continued, ' that since the little tabernacle was placed in your room you had had perfect freedom.'

" ' There is my despair ! ' cried Emma—' there is my despair ! Never had the demon dared to present himself in the presence of the ADORABLE ; and after great trouble, and many refusals, my confessor obtained leave to place HIM in my room, keeping the key himself. For a week I was in heaven ! I lay down at night with a soul so happy, and I could not sleep ; I needed not, for I felt fresh in the dear presence of my Saviour. He used to say to me. *Fear not !* Oh ! I am a sinner !—I am a sinner ! The night before last ! Oh, God ! My heart is breaking. I feel it ! I had not seen IT since I was in London—my God had protected me ! And the night before last I was as usual in my little bed and thinking on my God, and looking at the little lamp. Oh ! my heart began to beat. I looked on the floor. It stood there—there ! IT gnashed its teeth, and the fire flashed red from its murderous jaws, and IT crouched for the bound, and—O Saviour ! I called upon Jesus and Mary in vain, and Jesus so near me ! I am deserted because I am a sinner ! I am deserted ! Oh, God ! ' The Blessed Sacrament had been secretly removed.

" The obsession continued six months and a half. The girl's face and neck were wounded—one frightful collection of lacerations and scars. She had been driven mad. I saw her in that condition with my own eyes—black, torn, bleeding, and desperate. We formed a mixed jury of Protestants and Catholics. We brought the young lady to a room entirely denuded of furniture. We firmly nailed an arm-chair in the midst of this room. We put a straight-waistcoat on the young person, and a soldier's stock under her neck—this last precaution being taken to save her throat. We left her in a state of utter incapacity to stir body, hand, arm, or head. The left foot alone remained free, to enable her to give notice of any attack by knocking on the floor. We then taped the window-sashes and *sealed them.* We stopped the entrance to the chimney and *sealed it.* We locked the door, sealed the keyhole, and left her to her fate. We had not waited long when a knocking was heard overhead—we had retired to the room underneath. We slowly unsealed the keyholes. We unlocked the door and looked in. The sight was terrible. There was the poor young lady. Her face was black and livid; her eyes were fixed and glaring from beneath her brows. She frothed in convulsions, and spat forth blood and foam at every spasm. Her cheeks were laid open in wounds and bites. She appeared on the verge of a sudden death.

" The most wonderful part remains to be spoken. The confessor of the young lady was accompanied by two other clergymen ; and having by great exertion restored the poor thing, the room was prepared for Mass. At the close of the Mass the young lady received communion.

Shortly after the exorcism commenced. Turned towards the lady who knelt before him, while we stood witnesses of the deed, the clergyman took a large book in his hands, and, with a look like one who commanded earth and hell in the name of God, he raised his right hand aloft and made the sign of the Cross. Then he commanded the spirit to be gone ‘in the name of the Father, of the Son, and of the Holy Ghost’. The girl shrieked and tore away through the women who held her, as though she was flying from the embrace of fire. An amiable looking clergyman suggested to the exorcist to change the adjurations and to use some indifferent Latin words in the same tones of voice. Three times the priest pronounced the words of his Ritual, and at each adjuration she seemed flung into hell. Between each of them he pronounced some rules of syntax precisely in the same tone, and she lay comparatively calm and exhausted.

"I remarked precisely the same effects produced by blessed water. When the effects had been produced by blessed water, he substituted common water, and I assure you no change whatever followed the use of it. The clergymen then returned to the use of the blessed water, and having cast it upon her, she shrieked and bounded with the power of ten devils. [From that forward] the young lady remained calm, tranquil, and happy, and has so continued to this hour."—*Ailey Moore: a Tale of the Times*, by Father Baptist.

———

PART VIII.

SAFEGUARDS.

103. *Question.*—What are the safeguards against the demon's power?

Answer.—(1) *To trust in God, and to trust in Him un-*

boundedly.—God is the Sovereign Ruler and Preserver of all. In St. Matthew (vi. 25) our Blessed Lord says : " Be not solicitous for your life what you shall eat, nor for your body what you shall put on. Is not the life more than the meat, and the body more than the raiment? Behold the birds of the air ; for they neither sow, nor do they reap, nor gather into barns, and your heavenly Father feedeth them. Are not you of much more value than they ? "

(2) *To call on the holy Name of Jesus.*—St. Bernardine says : " When the Apostle Paul was rapt to the third heaven, and saw the Divine Essence, in that vision we may assume, that when he saw the glorious God in the glory of the Father, established in the heavenly places above principality, power, virtue, and domination, and above every name that shall be named in this world and the next, and when he saw Him in such sublimity of glory, enraptured with the sight, he exclaimed from his inmost heart : ' Jesus ! Jesus ! my Lord ! ' At the naming of that Name, and the utterance of that cry, all the heavenly citizens genuflected, adoring Jesus at the invocation of His holy Name. At that same invocation, he understood that the demons in hell prostrated themselves, as did also the souls of the Church suffering. And therefore it was that, returning from the heavens, and remembering what he saw, he wrote in the spirit of God commanding that ' in the name of Jesus every knee shall bow of those in heaven, on earth, and in hell '—the heavenly spirits by glory, the earthly spirits by grace, and the infernal spirits by everlasting justice adoring and honouring Him." —*Serm.* 49, Dominic Palm.

" But because it is unwillingly and with the utmost grudge

that the demons pay honour to this holy Name, it is therefore with the greatest hatred and loathing they hear it invoked, and therefore it ought to be ever devoutly and reverently on the lips of those who, through Him, have been saved" (Brognolo).

Upon the text: "And He gave them (the disciples) power over unclean spirits, that they would cast them out, and that they would heal every infirmity and disease"— upon the answer of "the 72," "they returning in joy said: Lord we have even cast out devils in Thy Name"—and upon our Blessed Lord's reply: "I have seen Satan, as lightning falling from heaven"—St. Bernard has this most encouraging comment. Speaking in the Name of our Blessed Lord he says: "Do not be astonished if the devils fear my Name and that it drive them out of men, when by its power Satan and his angels were expelled from heaven and fell rapid as the lightning into hell. This also is what is stated in the Apocalypse (chap. xii.). After the battle was waged in heaven between Michael and the dragon, and after he was overthrown, and cast into endless torments, the blessed of God rejoiced and cried: Now is Salvation and Power; that is, from the holy Name of Jesus has come a saving Power, and Virtue has gone out from His Christ." "Holy and terrible is His Name," says the Psalmist (chap. x.), *holy* indeed to His angels and the faithful on earth, but *terrible* to the demons.

We have examples, all through the ages of the Church, of demons being expelled at the invocation of the sacred Name.

In the Acts (chap. xvi.), we read that Paul expelled one of those demons from a Pythoness: "I order you," he said, "in the Name of Jesus Christ to depart from her. And he departed from her that hour."

St. Clement tells that St. Peter thus spoke to a demon: "I care not how you entered, but *in the Name* of Jesus Christ I order you to depart from the man".

Of St. John the Evangelist, we read that he said: "I interdict you *in the Name* of Jesus Christ that you dwell here any longer". And again: "*In the name* of Jesus Christ depart hence, and never again return ".

All the Fathers who have written of the holy Name, in their Homilies, Sermons, Treatises, or Meditations, have unanimously enlarged on this power of the sacred Name. Thus spoke St. Justin Martyr against Tryphon, Origen against Celsus, Tertullian on the Soldiers' Crown, St. Cyprian against Demetrius, and St. Athanasius, *de Incarn.*

St. Gregory writing on the text: "But the signs of those who will believe are those which follow. *In My Name* they shall cast out demons, they shall speak in strange tongues, they shall handle serpents, and if they shall taste anything deadly it shall not harm them. On the sick they shall lay their hands, and they shall recover." Mark (xvi.) says: "Whether are we to conclude because these things now rarely occur, that there is little or no faith? By no means. But these things were necessary in the beginning of the Church ; for when great crowds were being converted, it was necessary that their infant faith should be as it were nourished, just as we water young plants." This will answer an objection that some may raise as to the thing not being done so frequently in aftertimes as in the days of the Apostles; yet, anyone reading the Lives of the Saints and the more detailed histories of the Church will find innumerable examples.

St. Cyriacus, Deacon, when in prison for the faith, wrought many miracles; among the rest he freed by his prayers from the possession of the demon, Arthemia, daughter of Diocletian. Being sent to Sapor, King of Persia, he rescued his daughter, Jobia, from the possession of a nefarious spirit.—*Rom. Brev.*, Aug. 8.

St. Bernardine tells of the great St. Bernard that when he had come to Pavia from Milan, a certain man came to him, leading on his wife who was possessed by a demon. Then the demon through the woman's mouth began to cry out: "Not me from my betrothed will this feeder-on-herbs, this vegetable-eater, drive out". "It is not Bernard will drive you out," answered the Saint, "but it is our Lord Jesus Christ." By and bye, when the Saint was praying, the evil spirit cried: "Oh, willingly would I depart, but I cannot. The great Lord does not wish it." To whom the Saint made answer: "And who is the great Lord?" He replied: "Jesus the Nazarene". And then the man of God said: "Have you ever seen Him?" But he answered, "Yes". The Saint asked: "Where have you seen Him?" "In glory," was the reply. "And were you in glory?" asked the Saint. "Yes," answered the demon. (It must be understood not confirmed in glory.) "How then have you left it?" demanded Bernard. And he got for reply, uttered in a wailing tone: "Alas! many of us fell with Lucifer". Everybody standing by heard these replies coming from the mouth of the woman. Then the man of God put this query: "Would you wish to return?" But the demon, cackling in a most

awful manner, cried out : "Too late ! too late !" Then the
Saint prayed, and the demon departed from the woman.
But when the blessed Bernard had left, and was gone a
good distance away, the demon attempted to return again
into the woman, whereupon the woman's husband ran after
the Saint and told him what had happened. But he, having
taken a paper, cut it in the form of a circle, and wrote there-
on : "I order thee, demon, in the Name of our Lord Jesus,
that you never again attempt to touch this woman". This
he told the man to place around his wife's neck. He did
so, and the demon never ventured to harm her thereafter.

"But for the honour and glory of this holy Name, as also
for its utility to the faithful in general, it is well to add, that
this Name is given to men, not only to cast out devils, but
for many other purposes ; and hence our Blessed Lord, after
saying : "In my Name they shall cast out devils," immediately adds : "They shall speak in strange tongues, they
shall handle serpents," &c., &c. (Brognolo).

St. Bernardine says : "This most holy Name is a general
remedy for all who are ailing "—that is, who are ailing from
the evils brought on by original sin. "And hence in every
weakness, whether of body or of soul, arising from that, we
are to have recourse to the holy Name."

St. Peter Ravenna says : "This is the Name that has
given sight to the blind, hearing to the deaf, the power of
walk to the lame and the stricken, speech to the dumb, life
to the dead, and has put to flight even the whole power of
legions of demons over obsessed or possessed bodies".

St. Bernardine again says : "If any infirmity happens to
you or yours, do not cast aside proper or suitable remedies,

but at the same time have recourse to the most holy Name of Jesus. It often happens that natural remedies will not assist the sick, on account of the weakness of the person, or the strength of the disease, or the failure of properly diagnosing it, or that the sickness itself is irremediable of its own nature ; hence the faithful ought at once to fly to the feet of Jesus and have recourse to that holy Name, by whose efficacy demons are driven out, serpents handled, poisons nullified, and infirmities driven away." "Everyone who calleth on the Name of the Lord (Jesus) shall be saved" (*Acts* ii.).

St. Bernardine relates a singular story of St. Denis, the Areopagite, while he was still a pagan : " It happened that St. Paul was passing by Athens, and a blind man came before him. St. Denis, being still a pagan, said to the Apostle : If you will say to this blind man : In the name of my God open thy eyes and see, and that he shall see, I will at once believe in your teaching ; but in order that you may not use any magic arts, he continued : I will myself prescribe the form of words that you are to use. These, they shall be : In the Name of Jesus Christ, who was born of a virgin, was crucified, died, and was buried, who arose from the grave, and ascended into heaven, receive thy sight. Then Paul replied : That there might be no suspicion of foul play or magic arts, I wish that you yourself would use those very words you have spoken. St. Denis made use of the words : In the Name of the Lord Jesus, &c., I say to thee, blind man, receive thy sight ; and lo ! the blind man saw. And so," adds St. Bernardine, " many in our times, have experienced both in their own cases as well as in those of others " (*Sermon* 49, On the Name of Jesus).

(3) *To call on the most holy Name of Mary.*—" We embrace under one invocation the most noble persons of Jesus Christ our Lord, and of the most blessed Virgin Mary His mother. It surely is not fitting to separate those who have been united in the closest bonds both of nature and of grace " (Brognolo). Arnold Carnotensis says : " It is but one, the flesh of Mary and of Christ, but one spirit, and one charity, and therefore it was said by the angel : The Lord is with thee ". This the faithful understand, and hence in all their troubles and temptations they unite the sweet names of Jesus and Mary ; and the Church has solemnly sanctioned this in granting an indulgence of 25 days for saying : " Jesus and Mary ". The most august name of Mary signifies Queen, and she is Queen not alone of angels and of men, but of demons also ; and the demons are as obedient as any others to her.

St. Bernard says: " The demons not only fear the Blessed Virgin, but when they hear the name of Mary they tremble with dread ". And again : " Whenever the name of Mary is invoked, the evil power of the demon is warded off; because *Mary is terrible as an army set in battle array* ". And he gives the reason, when he writes on these words : " And she shall crush thy head ". Mary crushes the head of the serpent, when—the head being the seat of thought—she tramples on and destroys every malicious suggestion of the evil one.

In the *Revelations of St. Brigid* it is told : " All the demons venerate and fear this name, and when they hear her holy name they immediately depart from the soul which before they held possession of ".

St. Bonaventure says: "Not so much do men fear an army drawn up against them, arrayed in all the panoply of war, as the demons fear the invocation of Mary's name, or the power of her patronage. As wax melts and loses its natural strength and solidity when held to the fire, so the demons lose their brazen hardihood, wherever they find her sacred name frequently called upon, her patronage invoked, or her example followed."

St. Germanus, addressing the Blessed Virgin, says: "Thou, by the bare invocation of thy holy name, dost put to flight the attacks of the most virulent demon, and preservest safe and secure thy clients who devoutly invoke thee".

Denis, the Carthusian, says: "There are no souls so cold in divine love, that if they invoke the sacred name with a firm purpose of amending, that the devil will not depart from them".

Brognolo says: "It sometimes happens that our Blessed Lord Jesus will grant a favour more easily at the invocation of most holy Mary's name, than even at His own ".

St. Anselm says: "More quickly at times does salvation come at the invocation of the name of Blessed Mary, than even at that of her Divine Son: and this, not indeed that she is greater or more powerful than He ; nor is it through her that He is great and powerful, but she through Him. Wherefore, then, should it be that grace and favours will at times come to us more quickly through her than through Him? I say what I feel. Her Son is Lord of all, judging and discerning the merits of each. If, therefore, a sinner invokes His sacred Name, and He refuses to be instantly propitious, He acts as is just. But when the same sinner calls on Mary, and Mary presents herself instead of the sinner, then it is the Blessed Mary's merits, and not the sinner's merits that are weighed, and grace and repentance are granted. Thus does the Divine Son wish to show to men that through His most blessed Mother they may obtain all things."

St. Bernard cries out : " O happy and blessed Lady, whoever loves you honours God, who clings to you will never lose God, who calls upon your venerable name shall indubitably obtain whatever he asks ".

(4) *To rely upon the protection of the angels, but especially of our guardian angels.*—"Although the first duty of the angels is to praise God continually, and as ministers to stand before His throne, yet they do not disdain to perform various kind offices for men, such as protecting and curing them. These two acts of *protecting* and *curing* are typified in two great and prominent examples which we have in the Old Bible. Three times is St. Michael the great archangel introduced as combating Satan—in the Apocalypse, where is related the war in heaven ; in the Epistle of St. Jude ; and thirdly, where he guards the body of Moses. His name signifies *Who is like to God*—meaning, what enemy is powerful enough to injure those whom God protects. The second example is that of Raphael, who both protects and cures ; and his name signifies *The medicine of God*" (Brognolo).

The angels protected Jacob when he returned from Mesopotamia and met his brother ; and the book of Genesis calls the place *Mahanias*—that is, the place of encampment or protection.

In the fourth book of Kings it is told that Eliseus, being

sought after by the king of Syria, was protected by those blessed spirits, which appeared in the form of fiery steeds.

In the book of Judges Deborah sings : " From heaven was war waged against them ; the stars standing in order fought against Sisara in their course ". Did lightnings or fiery darts come from heaven, or did the sun and moon and stars leave their places and fight against the uncircumcised ? and if not, how can she say that heaven waged war against Sisara ? Surely it was by the hand of a woman—to denote most ignominous defeat—that a nail was driven from one temple to the other of Sisara, and he was fastened to the earth ?

Jacobus Alvarez says : " The heavens wage war against our enemies for us, when it sends us help, which as lightning flashes or darts of fire break up and overthrow the ranks of the enemy ". " Thus plainly is it seen that the Israelites were delivered by angels from the hands of their enemies ; and hence it is that Deborah sings, and Barac with her : ' Heaven has warred in our favour,' *i.e.*, the power of God has defended us ; and ' the stars standing in their order and their course,' *i.e.*, the angels while standing before the throne of God, contemplating His Divine Essence, and never removed from the enjoyment of the Beatific Vision, fought against Sisara " (Brognolo).

The Abbot Rupert says : " The stars standing in their order and their course fight for men when they terrify and put to flight the demons attacking or rising up against them ".

In the book of Machabees it is told that Judas Machabeus, finding himself with a handful of men opposed to a large army, begged of God to be his protection. Wherefore, we read: "When the battle was hottest, there appeared to his adversaries five men coming from heaven, of beautiful aspect, riding on golden horses, and affording protection to the Jews. Of these, two keeping Machabeus in their midst, and shielding him with their arms, preserved him safe. Into the ranks of his adversaries, however, they cast darts and flames of light, by which they were so confused, and by blindness, that they turned their backs and were slain in the greatest rout and disorder."

In the *Lives of the Fathers of the Desert* it is related that the Abbot Moses, being very much tormented and harassed by a demon, came to the Abbot Isidore to ask for a remedy. They talked for some time about spiritual things, and the Abbot Moses became quiet. Then, at the orders of Isidore, they went on the roof of the cell, when he told the Abbot Moses to turn his eyes to the west, and there he saw an immense multitude of demons, all in fury, and brandishing weapons as if ready to do battle. Then he told him to look to the east, and there he saw a glorious host of angels, with countenances reflecting the beauty of heaven. "Behold," said Isidore, "those that are to the west are they that would attack and smite us, those to the east are the angels whom God sends to shield and protect us." The holy Abbot was by this vision comforted and encouraged, and putting his trust in the protection of his guardian-angel, he was never molested any more by the demon.

"He hath given His angels charge over thee, that they guard thee in all thy ways" (*Ps.* xc.).

St. Augustine says: "These are the citizens of the heavenly Jerusalem, the blessed city, which is our mother on high, and they are sent down (by that mother) for the sake of those who have received the inheritance of salvation, *that they would preserve them from their enemies,* and guard them in all their ways ".

Venerable Bede says in his comment on St. Luke : " Since the unclean spirits are everywhere engaged in destroying peace, the Lord God has constituted for our protection an army of angels whose presence and protection overcomes the hardihood of the demons ".

St. Basil says : " As the walls of a city protect it on all sides, and ward off the fiercest attacks of its enemies, so God's angels, at your back and your breast, guard you round. And lest any portion should remain unguarded, a thousand shall fall on your left hand and ten thousand on your right ; but the Lord God has given His angels orders that they guard thee in all thy ways."

St. Chrysostom, on St. Matthew (chap. xxi.), says : " What is this foss that guards the vineyard round ? What but the angels in their course guarding the people of God, lest the invisible robbers should break into the vineyard. These are the guardians looking over the walls, that protect the city of Jerusalem and its flocks through the watches of the night, lest, like a lion, the enemy should hurry off with souls when there was no one to rescue them."

St. Laurence Justinian says : " The angels ward off the demons, so that they cannot injure whomsoever they wish. For, were it not for angelical protection, I ask you who could combat and overcome the rage of such virulent and savage beasts, who avoid their traps, repel their temptations, or detect their evils ? Truly those good angels hedge round our path, lest we strike the foot of the soul against the rock of scandal or the stone of offence.

104. *Question.*—Have the angels more power to succour and serve us than the demons have to harm us?

Answer.—It must be remembered that the angels are divided into nine choirs, that each angel of a superior choir has naturally more power than the individual angels of an inferior choir. Now, the same power that the demons had before their fall, the same power they possess even still. Therefore, naturally, that is, if God does not otherwise ordain, some of the demons have more power than some of our guardian angels; because some of the fallen angels were originally in a higher choir or order. But God does ordain otherwise.

In the first place, then, we answer, that were they of the same choir or order originally, the desire of the good angel to benefit is more vehement, and therefore more effectual, than the malice or enmity of the evil one to do us harm.

Again, even though they were of a different order, the good angel has more power than the evil one; for the good angel has God behind him, the evil one has none.

" And by good right are they called *Medici* (healing or curing angels), for they are *far more solicitous and far more powerful to do us service in our needs* than the demons are to do us injury. And the reason is: Because the good angels, though of their nature inferior (that is, originally) to the bad angels (and consequently subject to them), yet by another order of nature they command those superior demons, because the power of the divine justice to which the good angels adhere is infinitely beyond the natural

strength of any angels, and consequently can work great
wonders. Again, much more solicitous is he in his works
who expects rewards from his industry, than he who is sure
that the harder he works the sharper will his punishment be.
Now, the angels receive accidental glory from their good
guardianship, and the wicked angels obtain for themselves
but an increase of punishment " (Brognolo).

It is not to be doubted that the good angels receive joy,
and therefore happiness and (accidentally) additional glory
—" there is more joy in heaven," &c.—but it is generally
held now that in hell there is no increase or decrease of pain.
The master of St. Bonaventure, Alexander Alensis (*de Ang.*,
q. 41), St. Thomas (3, p. q. 113), as well as St. Bonaventure
himself (in 2, d. II., art. 2, q. 2) seem however to favour the
position of Brognolo, that demons receive an additional
share of accidental pain.

"Wherefore," continues the old Franciscan Father, "if
the demons at the invocation or command of magicians,
sorcerers, &c., bring various evils on human bodies, on the
other hand the angels at the will of the Blessed Virgin, the
Saints, and holy servants of God (God so designing) bring
various benefits not alone to the souls of men, but even to
their bodies, by curbing or expelling various evil and noxious
humours, and by exciting healthy and useful ones instead,
by healing scars and wounds, and by preserving the body
and its organs from disease."

Petrus Blessensis goes so far as to say, that as parents
when children are sick grow more affectionate and attentive,
so the good angels show more solicitude for those that are
weak, than for those that are well (*Serm.*, de Angelis).

105. *Question.*—If, then, everyone has an angel guardian, how is it possible that some are harassed by the demon?

Answer.—By way of reply, let us ask a question: If God be everywhere, and God is everywhere,—if, furthermore, God be more powerful than the demon, and God is more powerful than the demon,—how comes it to pass that any man is at all attacked by the demon? These are God's ways.

But let us hear an old Florentine theologian, Joseph Angles, in answer. " This, at any rate, does not arise from any want of caution on the part of our holy guardians; for, not to speak of just souls, all theologians confess that the angels do not wholly abandon even the most hardened sinners. But it happens, either because we repel them ourselves, or we will not listen to their counsels and inspirations; or because they cannot work for us against our perverse will; or again, because God does not permit them, perhaps on account of justice or punishment, or for our better illumination, or that we might be taught to cast ourselves more fully on His ever-watchful providence, and that He intends after a time to overwhelm us with gifts on account of the annoyance and struggles to which He has willed us to be temporarily subjected." The holy angels are therefore to be daily invoked by all.

106. *Question.*—Do the just in heaven assist us against the demons?

Answer.—St. John in the Apocalypse (chap. v.) describes the blessed in heaven as *holding harps,* and *having golden phials in their hands.*

With their harps they praise God, and while they praise the most glorious Lord, they not only serve and worship Him, but they even do battle against our adversaries for us. David says so (*Ps.* cxlix.) : "The praises of God on their lips, and double-edged swords in their hands, *that they might bind kings in fetters, and the nobles of them in manacles of iron* ".

St. Basil says : "These are they who, as towers, are our strength and our refuge against the enemy. O Sacred Choir (of martyrs) ! *O universal guardians of the human race !* Ye are our ambassadors with the most powerful Lord ! Ye are the stars of the world, and the blooming roses of the Church."

" But phials they hold in their hands, that they might confer benefits on men; for they are full of odours and medicines, which can heal all infirmities. For what disease is there so obstinate or dangerous that it shall not recede at the prayers of the saints ? " (Brognolo).

In the life of that young virgin and martyr, St. Agatha, we read that when she had been severely wounded and then cast into prison, an old man appeared to her that night, lighting up by the effulgence of his presence the darkness of her prison, and he told her he was sent to cure her. "Who are you," said Agatha, "that comest to cure me ? " "I am the Apostle of Christ," the old man replied. "Be not suspicious of me, daughter; for He it was that sent me whom thou dost love in thy heart and with thy most pure soul. I am His Apostle, and in His Name remember Thou shalt be cured." And when she was cured the Saint said : "I bless thee, O God, Father of my Lord Jesus Christ, and give Thee thanks, because Thou hast been mindful of me, and hast sent Thy Apostle to cure my wounds" (*Roman Brev.*, Feb. 5). Now the Apostle was of course dead at the time.

(5) *Recourse to fasting.*—In the Old Bible numerous examples are to be found of the utility of fasting—in the book of Judith, in the book of Esther, in the book of Daniel, in the books of Kings, in the book of Jonas.

St. Basil says: "Even our Blessed Lord in His combat with the demon did not allow that flesh which He took on Himself for our sakes to be tempted until He had first prepared it by fasting. At all times fasting is useful, nor will the demon attempt to attack the person that fasts. *Fasting gives arms sufficient to combat a whole legion of demons.*"

St. Chrysostom says: "Against the nature of demons is constituted the power of fasting". And again: "Fasting supplies arms against the demon".

St. Ambrose says: "We have our camps of safety—they are our fasts, which secure us against the attacks of the demon. Fasting is a wall of brass for the Christian, warding off the demon and excluding the foe; for the devil is frightened at the paleness of the cheek, is discouraged at the weakness of the constitution, and totally banished by the hunger of the body." And again: "A more powerful weapon against the wily serpent you cannot find than the fasting of the body".

Tertullian says: "Fasting is our shield to fling back the enemy's darts".

Origen says: "When you fast, you overcome the demons,

and put to flight all their class, their suggestions and temptations ".

St. Jerome says : " Beautiful is the spotless virgin that terrifies the demons : that virgin is fasting ".

St. Anthony : " Believe me, Satan fears the watchings and fastings of the pious soul ".

Our Blessed Lord : " This class of demons is not to be cast out but by prayer and fasting ".

(6) *The Sacraments of our Blessed Lord.*—It is said that contraries are cured by contraries ; if, therefore, the demon takes sensible forms and makes use of sensible things to injure man temporarily and eternally, what wonder that the Sacraments should have from our Blessed Lord, the opponent and conqueror of the demon, effects, even temporary effects, which would neutralise the malice of the evil one ?

It is said in the Psalms (ch. lxxiii.) : " *In the midst of the waters* thou shalt crush the heads of the dragons " ; and in the waters of baptism the demon is crushed. In the prayers of the Ritual it is said : " Depart from him, thou unclean spirit, and give place to the Holy Spirit, the Comforter " ; and the Church, to show its contempt of him, puts him out with a breath from the priest's lips.

In the year 1596 a Gentile lady was possessed by a demon. It was told to her, that until she became a Christian she could not be freed from him. Thereupon she gave her consent to become a Christian, and had herself instructed and prepared for baptism. On the night previous to her receiving it, the demon came to her and said, " Are we going to be parted now after so long a friendship ? Very well; but you shall not go scot-free. Your beautiful hair that you prided in I will lop off;" and taking a scissors he clipped the hair from her head, and tore her hair to pieces. Next day, however, she persisted in her purpose, received baptism, and was never afterwards molested by the demon.

Another example.—There was a young man, a pagan. The demon frequently appeared to this young man in the shape of a huge dog, all hair, and exceedingly fierce-looking. The dog regularly spoke to him, and in spite of the young man carried him into the mountain fastnesses and kept him there several days. While there he tormented him in ways that would be shocking to relate. The young man had an inspiration. He fled one day to the church, and there hearing it explained what power God and His Church had over the demons, he got himself baptised, and was never more assaulted by the demon.

In the year 1549 a poor maidservant was most grievously tormented by a demon. Every night the evil spirit came in the shape of a black vulture with huge wings, and bore away in its talons the poor terrified girl from her bed. She was then a pagan, but on her being baptised she was saved from his assaults. These examples are given by F. Ludovicus Frois in his Japan letters.

I will give one example, which may be not alone interesting but useful to my brethren on the mission, and which I heard from the lips of one of the most revered and learned ecclesiastics in Ireland. A child was brought to the chapel to be baptised. The priest rightly asked if the child had been baptised privately, and on learning that the child had been privately baptised by the midwife, a correct and

respectable woman, the priest went through the ceremonies
as ordered by the Ritual, omitting to baptise it conditionally,
and the child was carried home. But some unaccountable
sickness seemed to have taken possession of it. It worked
at times in convulsions, that were pitiable and horrible to
see. It was taken to doctors, rounds were paid at holy
wells, masses were even said,—but all to no use. At last,
after proper advice, the priest had it conditionally baptised,
when the convulsions ceased, and the child recovered its
natural strength, and never after suffered an attack.

Confirmation seems even still more calculated to save us
from the attacks of the demon, as it, by its seven gifts, gives
us that fulness of faith and trust in God, and that strength
and courage as soldiers, so necessary to combat the evil one.

In the Second Book of Thomas of Canterbury, chap. lvii.,
is the following : " The Bishop of London, the venerable
Bonifacius " (writes Thomas), " told once in my presence that
there was in a certain town a blind man. This blind man,
by some compact with the evil one, was enabled to herd all
the cows of the hamlet. He could drive them out in the
morning, keep them from the crops, select proper grounds
for them, tell whether they were white, or black, or brown,
and such other things as were absolutely beyond the power
of a blind man. On the occasion of the bishop's visiting
the place, this man was struck with remorse for having
bartered eternal light for a temporary advantage, and having
confessed and received confirmation, and renounced all
agreements for the future with the evil one, he lost the
extraordinary power that he before had, lived a most
edifying life, and died a holy death."

Penance.—If the demon exercise his power for sin and because of sin, then the Sacrament of Penance which cleanses and drives out all sin, and brings the grace of God into the soul, is exceedingly well calculated to banish the demon from the soul of man.

In the life of St. Gregory, John the deacon relates that there were three persons who were attacked by the demon, and who came to confession to St. Gregory, and that two of the three were immediately cured. The third person came again and again, and as many as eight times, and yet the demon did not depart, because each confession was bad. Being terrified by the continual assaults of the evil one, the penitent at length, on the ninth turn, disclosed the hidden sin, which was a sin of theft, received absolution, and, returning home, was never more molested.

The Blessed Eucharist.—"As lions breathing fire we should return from that holy table, objects of terror to the demons" (St. Chrysostom).

In the life of St. Paul of the Cross, we read: "When he was occupied with a mission in a place called Rio, a poor woman came to him, who was ill-treated by her husband on account of the calumnies of another woman. Paul sent for this other woman, and persuaded her to retract what she had said. He then sent for the husband, and when he had come, Paul said to the calumniator: 'Now is the time to unsay what you had falsely accused this good man's wife of. Was it not all false?' She fell away at once, and replied: 'No, no; it was perfectly true, every word'. Paul then said: 'Very well; come with me before the Blessed Sacrament, and repeat that'. She did so, and repeated it with an oath.

Scarcely were the perjured words out of her mouth, when she was seized by an invisible power, raised in the air, and carried outside the church. Her tongue was hanging from her mouth black as ink, and her whole face became livid and horrible. Paul exorcised the evil spirit, and after some time the demon let the wretch fall half-stunned upon the pavement. The Saint then took the Ciborium from the tabernacle, and blessed her with it. She recovered, and with great sorrow confessed her sins, and retracted all her calumnies."

Extreme Unction is so called because it is usually the extreme or last Sacrament in which anointing is given to the body. The Church wishes it to be understood that one of the natural effects arising from it is the restoration of bodily health. Now the sickness of the body may result from many causes, and a possible one is the evil action of the demon. In St. Mark (chap. vi.) we read: "And going forth they preached the doctrine of penance, and they cast out many demons, and they anointed with oil many that were sick, and they were cured".

(7) *The Sacramentalia.*— By sacramentalia are meant things blessed by the Church, such as sacred images, crosses, medals, gospels, agnus deis, images of the saints, holy water, &c., &c., which have not of course the same virtue, efficacy, or grace as the sacraments; but which nevertheless are sacred, and by the blessing of the Church have a special power of their own. They are called sacramentalia, because of their resemblance to the sacraments in this, that sensible objects are the indirect, not the direct, as in the sacraments, means of grace. Some people attribute to them a power

which is little less than superstitious—they treat them as if they were charms. In this they do wrong. Others laugh at them. This is wrong also. The Church blesses them, and it begs of God, that where these sacramentalia be kept, as sacred pictures for instance, or when they are piously used in a certain way, as the sprinkling of holy water, that they have a certain effect, and that the blessing of God be on that person, that house, family, or place. Those who laugh at and mock them, then laugh at the prayers of the Church, which no Catholic should do. Those who give them charmed or superstitious power attribute to them a virtue they do not possess. "Their dignity appears in this, that all of them are holy, either that because of themselves they are calculated to lead to holiness, or they are instituted and intended by the Church to lead to holiness" (Brognolo).

"Their efficacy is both internal and external—internal, because, when assisted by the action of the person himself (*ex opere operantis*), they take away venial sins, by exciting to acts of contrition or love, by which venial sins are directly and immediately taken away; externally, by conferring temporal or spiritual benefits, or warding off the attacks of the demon or his agents" (St. Bonaventure).

I will briefly state what are the effects of the *sacramentalia* as theology teaches. The sacramentalia are six in number, or six species, which are given in this way :—

1, Orans; 2, Tinctus; 3, Edens; 4, Confessus; 5, Dans; 6, Benedicens—(praying, sprinkling, eating, confessing, giving, blessing).

1, Prayer made in a consecrated church; 2, Holy water; 3, Eating anything blessed by the approved ritual of the

Church; 4, The confitior said at Mass or in the Office; 5, Giving (as for instance) alms; 6, The blessing of a bishop for example.

Now the effects of them. First, they do not remove mortal sins, nor even venial sins directly, but they are the means of obtaining great helps and graces from God, which enable a person, or which move a person, to make more frequent acts of contrition or charity or acts of the other virtues, or which dispose a soul to receive the sacraments more fittingly. If the sacramentalia had not some such effect, they would be but vain ceremonies. As, for instance, if prayer outside in the open field, *ceteris paribus*, were equal to prayer in a consecrated church, then the labour of consecration and the ritual and prayers were all vain and idle.

St. Thomas says that the sacramentalia can obtain the remission of venial sins, when their use is accompanied by an act of detestation of sin, such as the confitior, striking of the breast, the sprinkling of holy water; but St. Thomas takes care to add, that these do not of their own power remove sin, they but incline the mind to acts of sorrow or love.

To their use the Roman Pontiff may attach indulgences which would add a further merit to our own, and by which some of our just punishment may be wiped away.

Lastly, "they have the effect of repelling tempests, warding off harm, and expelling and coercing the devils" (Bonal).

The Crucifix.—By the sign of the cross the demons are driven away.

St. Paul says (*Col.* ii.): "Taking away the handwriting that was against us   and *despoiling principalities and powers*, He confidently gave Himself up, openly triumphing over them in Himself". He surely would not have triumphed over them, if He were not able to curb their malicious power.

St. Athanasius says: "The sign of the cross takes away all magic".

The Saints made use of this holy sign to perform most wonderful works—to take away disease, to extinguish fires, to calm tempests, to avert calamities, but especially to banish the demons, with all their arts, works, and wiles (see their holy lives).

Of St. Eligius, it is related that he used to say to his disciples: "Christians cannot be hurt by augury or any kind of magic, for wheresoever the sign of the cross with reverence and faith in God shall have preceded, there no enemy can approach to do harm".

The Patriarch, St. Eutychius, used to call the holy cross *a dart dreaded by the demons.*

St. Anthony, Abbot, used to dare the demons: "If you can, why do you not attack me? If one of you can harm me, why do you come to me in crowds? But you know that the sign of the cross and my faith in God are as a wall round about me, which you hate to see and are afraid to approach."

St. Gregory, Pope, relates a story, showing how in the mouth of persons not Christians even, it puts demons to flight: "A certain man from the Roman Campagna, a Jew, came to Rome, and was passing the night in the temple of Apollo. He was awakened by a terrible noise, and saw around him a host of evil spirits. He signed himself with the sign of the cross, and the devils fled away shouting half mockingly, half-terrified: 'Vah, vah, an empty vessel thou art, but signed!'"

St. Gregory Nazianzen relates another, which shows in a more striking manner the power of the sign of the cross: "The Apostate Julian was once invited by a magician to be present at a nightly meeting of the demons. Being affrighted by the noise, he had instant recourse," says Gregory, "to his old practice which he had abandoned, the sign of the cross, and by this he triumphed over his tormentors."

Even the demons themselves declare their fear of this most holy sign. Being expelled on one occasion by St. Patapius, they cried: "Truly terrible Thou art, O Nazarene —terrible Thou art, and everywhere holdest power and empire. Whither shall we go? If into the city—if into the desert—there Thou art before us, and by the bare sign of Thy cross, and the sole invocation of Thy Name, Thou drivest us away."

St. Ephrem, encouraging every one to make use of this most salutary sign, says: "We Christians are distinct from Jews and Gentiles, and our door-posts we surmount and crown with the most precious and life-giving crucifix, saying with the Apostle: 'God forbid that we should glory save in the cross of our Lord Jesus Christ'. But let us imprint that most saving sign not only on our doors, but on our foreheads, in our hearts, on our lips, on every sense and member of our body. Let us arm ourselves with this unconquerable weapon of the Christian, for when our adversaries, powerful though they be, even as all hell together, see this sacred sign, they depart in terror and confusion."

The Holy Gospels.—St. Paul says : "I do not blush at the Gospel ; for it is the power of God unto salvation to every believer, to Jew first, and Greek afterwards ".

It is a most pious custom, either to recite portions daily of the holy Gospel, or to have them about one either in print or in writing ; as if faithfully and piously borne they are of great assistance in driving away the demons.

" And first, this is plain from the practice of the Church, which orders, during holy Mass, the sacred Gospels to be publicly read ; and this also with many hidden and instructive ceremonies. For instance, it orders the deacon to turn to the North. *From the North*, says the Prophet Jeremias, *comes every evil* (chap. i.). Hence the Spouse, as if protecting the garden of the beloved from something foul and impure, wishes to drive it off. Very rightly, says William Mimatensis, is the Gospel read against the devil, that by its power it would expel him, for the devil hates the Gospel " (Brognolo).

At exorcisms the Gospel is customarily read by orders of the Church, and this shows what is the Church's belief regarding its power over the evil one.

" The Gospel kept in writing is also most useful in thwarting charms and magic " (Brognolo).

St. Barnabas, who was of the Apostolic College, cured many sick by ordering them to wear a Gospel beneath their dress.

St. Simeon wrote a Gospel and hung it round the neck of a sorceress, whom at once the evil spirit deserted, so that the woman never after phrensied or divined.

St. Anthony expelled a demon that was haunting a man

by writing a portion of the Scriptures on parchment and inserting it in the man's dress.

It was always, and is still, a custom with Christians to write the commencement of the Gospel of St. John as an epitome of the whole Gospels, enclose it in leather or linen, and wear it as people wear an Agnus Dei or Scapular.

107. *Question.*—From what has " a Gospel " its protecting power ?

Answer.—It is not from the blessing of the Church, for it is not blessed. Anyone may copy out a portion of the Gospel as it is to be found in the Bible or at the end of the Prayers at Mass in prayer-books, and then wrap it up and wear it. It has its protecting power from the fact that these are the inspired words of God—that these words are holy, because they tell about Jesus, and especially about that time when He publicly taught and instructed men, when He fought and conquered the demons, and redeemed us. Our wearing the Gospel, then, is a silent profession of our faith in Jesus Christ, a reverence for His holy Word, and an appeal to Him by that holy Gospel that He would, " out of Sion, protect us from harm ". Our protection then will be in proportion to our faith in our Blessed Lord, our reverence for His holy Word, and the earnestness of our heart's appeal to Him.

" And not only the words of the Gospel and the sacred Name of God, but also extracts from other parts of the Testament, from the Apostles' Creed, and from other prayers of the Church, are most useful in this respect " (Brognolo).

In the *Chronicles of the Friars Minors*, it is related that a certain Portuguese lady, being possessed by the devil, and grievously tormented by him, and being urged continually to commit suicide, invoked in her distress the intercession of St. Anthony of Padua. He appeared to her during sleep and said : " Read the writing that is hidden in thy bosom, and you will be afflicted no more ". The lady arose, and found there a slip of paper, containing the following words from the Office of the Church :

Ecce ✠ Crucem Domini, fugite partes adversae
Vicit Leo de tribu Juda, radix David. Alleluia, Alleluia.
(Behold the Cross of the Lord—away ye adverse powers—
He hath conquered, the Lion of Judah's tribe, the root of David's stock.
Alleluia, Alleluia.)

She quickly read, and piously kissed it, and that moment the demon left her. This writing, after the lady's death, was, by the orders of Dionysius, king of Portugal, preserved in the royal archives of the kingdom.

In the year 1843, there was in the Carmelite convent at Tours, in France, a holy nun named Sister Ste. Pierre: "This pious sister, in order to honour the Divine Child, got copies made of the Gospel read on the Feast of the Circumcision, and which is very short. These she enclosed in wrappers, and distributed among her acquaintances whom she knew to be devout to the holy Name of Jesus. M. Dupont also made many copies, and helped the good sister to distribute them. This is the Gospel known as the little Gospel of the Sister Ste. Pierre. These Gospels were carried to the sick, and wonderful cures and conversions were obtained through their means." (*Vie de M. Dupont*, p. 148. M. Dupont died in the year 1876, in the odour of sanctity.)

The Agnus Dei.—Agnus Deis, as commonly known, are

small particles or portions of consecrated wax enclosed in
leather or linen, and worn round the neck, or inserted in
one's scapulars or in one's clothes. The words *Agnus Dei*
mean Lamb of God, and the wax is called *Agnus Dei* wax,
because it has the impression of a lamb stamped on it at
the time it is blessed. It is blessed by the Pope, and by
him only—and blessed only once in every seven years. It
is always blessed on the first year, too, of the Pope's acces-
sion. The blessing has many mystical prayers. The Pope
begs of God that those who wear it piously and devoutly
should be delivered from all dangers, and in particular
from all wiles, temptations, and assaults, bodily and mentally,
of the enemy ; that the demons would be warded off and
terrified by the sign of the Cross and the figure of the Lamb,
typical of our Saviour Jesus Christ, impressed upon it, and
that the good angels from heaven surround and guard the
person that wears it.

" It is certain that these prayers are heard, and that they
have their effect, because they are poured forth in the
sight of the Lord by him who stands in the person of Jesus
Christ on this earth, and especially when the special blessing
of the Pontiff is attached to them, which is never unavailing,
as theologians commonly teach " (Brognolo).

Some vulgarly attribute to the wearing of the Agnus Dei
an infallible effect which it does not possess ; as, for instance,
a person going to cross the seas puts on an Agnus Dei, and
says he cannot be drowned. Now it has not the effect of
absolutely saving from shipwreck or drowning. Of itself, it
had not that effect, and the Pope never prayed that absolute
effect for it. Indeed, if an Agnus Dei had that effect, no

one would go to sea without one, and no one would be drowned. All the Pope prays for, and all, therefore, that can be vouched for, is, that God would thereby extend a special protection to persons in imminent danger ; and, of course, among the persons in very great danger are persons on a sea-voyage.

" Wherefore these waxen forms, consecrated by prayers and benedictions, are efficacious not alone against light-nings, storms, burnings, and such like, but also against the demons' power " (Brognolo).

The Relics of the Saints.—The souls of the saints are with Christ in heaven ; He has clothed them with everlasting bliss. Their bodies that are far away on the earth He will one day bring to heaven, and these too He will clothe in glory and bliss unfading. But until then will He have nothing to say to them ? Are they lost to Him—the bones of the sacred dead—just as they are lost to relatives and friends on this earth ? Is there no reward for them until the great recording day comes round ? Or, will He permit those dead bones to serve Him even still ? Surely there is a fitness in God's investing the bones—corporal things though they be—of the sainted dead with such power and awe, because they had during life served Him, as to drive away in terror and confusion those fallen creatures of His who in their day of trial disobeyed and defied Him—although, in their original state, the vanquished be indefi-nitely beyond their victors. It shows, moreover, God's great power, and the great power of His Christ, as well as demonstrating the contempt in which He holds the infernal hosts, that by His will things which are but dead dust and ashes, the very slime of the earth, should overcome and rout those splendid aerial beings whose luminous birth was before and beyond the stars.

St. John Damascene calls the relics of the saints "fountains of aid, from which numberless benefits come to us".

Sometimes it happens that not alone a portion of their flesh or bone, but even the clothes or garments that touched them, or handkerchiefs dipped in their blood, are endowed by God with wonderful power. Thus does God honour those bodies that served Him in life. Sometimes, too, there exudes an oil or balsam or sacred liquor from the dead body, which has given sight to the blind, hearing to the deaf, and performed many other preternatural cures.

In the *Roman Breviary*, 1st Aug., we read : " In the year 969, a certain count, companion to the Emperor Otho, was possessed by an unclean spirit, so that this poor man tore and ate his own flesh. The Emperor ordered him to be taken to the Pope ; and upon the Holy Father putting the sacred chains of St. Peter round his neck, the evil spirit broke forth from the count's body, and never after molested him."—Feast of St. Peter, *Ad Vincula.*

" Whence has arisen the custom to pay public worship to these relics, to encase them in sacred shrines, to keep lamps burning before them, to have processions, feasts, and patterns in their honour ; thus, in the first place, to give glory to God, who gave such glory to weak, humble creatures, and, in the second place, to beg the protection of those holy servants of God, whose relics these are " (Brognolo).

108. *Question.*—What honour is it proper to pay to relics ?

Answer.—When relics are solemnly exposed for veneration, it is fitting and proper to go down on one's knees, and adore God in the first place, and then reverence the relics that are solemnly exposed. If they repose in the church of the saint the same honour is paid them.

If they are not solemnly exposed, but encased privately in a shrine—if (1) it be a relic belonging to our Blessed Lord—a portion of the true cross, for instance, one of the sacred nails, some of the crown of thorns, &c.—we genuflect before it, not to adore, but to exceedingly honour it; but if (2) it be a relic of a saint, or some holy thing that has merely touched the cross or nails or crown of thorns, then we uncover our heads and reverently bow before it, and honour the relic or sacred thing, as belonging to a great servant of God, or as something very holy.

109. *Question.*—Have sacred pictures any power against the demon ?

Answer.—Yes. In the first place, a reverence shown to the images of the saints is most pleasing to God, does honour to the saints, and consequently must be strongly efficacious against the enemy of God and His saints. In the next place, a reverence of them is calculated to bring great blessings on the persons who practise it, and on the house or parish where it is practised ; and, on the other hand, irreverence is frequently followed with severe chastisements. " The images of these saints, but especially that of the Blessed Virgin, are so hateful to the demons that they can scarcely bear to look upon them " (Brognolo). St. Augustine relates that a very holy nun who was grievously tormented by the demon was freed from his molestation by a picture of St. Jerome.

In the *Spiritual Meadow* it is told that a certain religious man prayed every day before an image of our Blessed Lady. On one occasion he was attacked by a most violent temptation, and this continued for some weeks. Harassed and wearied, he was praying to be delivered from it, when the devil openly appeared to him, and desired to enter into a compact with him to the following effect, that he would never trouble the man with this temptation any more, if the religious on his part would cease honouring the religious picture. On this the religious flung himself on his knees before the holy picture, lifted up his hands to heaven, and declared that henceforth he would pay it ten times more honour daily; and then he called on the holy Mother of God from his inmost heart to help him, when the devil was put to flight and the evil temptation ceased.

Holy Water.—There is a common saying in almost every language to the effect that the "devil hates holy water," thus showing the universal opinion of the faithful regarding its power in the matter of warding off demons. Its frequent use at the church door, in the oratory, in the Christian's bedroom, its being sprinkled on almost everything that the Church blesses, has made it take its place beside the Mass, the Sacraments, and the Rosary beads, as one of the distinctive properties of the Catholic religion.

In the fourth book of Kings (chap. v.) is related the story of Naaman, the Syrian, how he was cured of his leprosy by bathing in the waters of the Jordan, "though there were rivers in Damascus". In the same book (chap. ii.) the

Prophet blesses salt, and cures the waters of their barrenness. "And he healed the waters, and there was no longer in them either death or barrenness."

In the New Testament (*John* v.) is told the miraculous power of the pond Probatica. In the life of Sister Emmerich, it is told that one morning, when a child, coming home from early Mass, the devil met her, and struck her on the face. The cheek became very swollen, and she suffered intense pain, but the pain instantly ceased and the swelling subsided in her cheek when she applied holy water to it.

The Church grants 100 days' indulgence for making the sign of the cross while sprinkling oneself with holy water.

Dr. Murray, late Professor of Theology in Maynooth College, strongly recommended that the bed of the sick should be sprinkled with holy water frequently, not alone at the time of the priest's visit, or when the Sacraments were to be administered, but that the attendants should be advised and encouraged to sprinkle it often, and that a vessel containing holy water should be placed within reach of the sick person, so that when desirous he may sprinkle himself.

St. Theresa, the great Spanish ascetic and theologian— she who could so miraculously tell where the Blessed Sacrament was preserved, even though there was nothing outwardly to indicate Its presence, says of holy water : " I have experienced over and over that there is nothing which so quickly drives away the demons as holy water, and prevents them so surely from returning. So everyone ought to have great faith in holy water. I have received such consolation and comfort by it that I cannot find words to explain how it strengthens and fortifies the soul. And this is not imagination, for I have often experienced it. I feel as if I were hot and thirsty, and that a draught of cool water were given to me. Oh, there is not the smallest or slightest thing in the ordinance of the Church that is not a matter of wonder, since a few simple words of blessing can make such a difference between water that is blessed and water that is not."— Her Life, written by herself, chap. xxxi.

In the blessing of holy water, the Church prays: " In whatsoever house or dwelling of the faithful this water shall have been sprinkled, may it be free from all evil influence and escape all harm ; may no pestilent spirit abide there, and no infectious breath dwell in it ; all the treacherous snares of the enemy be far removed from it ; and should there be anything in it marring the happiness and security of the household, may it be driven far away, and peace and joy, together with the invocation of Thy holy Name, tranquilly dwell therein ".

This present age seems to look very sceptically on the power of holy water, and on the truth of that text of St. Peter, where he describes the devil going about like a roaring lion. Now, it is well to impress it on the mind that both these things are just as true in this our day as they were in the first ages of the Church. In the life of M. Dupont, the saintly layman of Tours, who died on the 18th March, 1876, in the odour of sanctity, it is told: " At the school of St. Martin, M. Dupont had learned to combat the enemy of the human race with all the weapons that faith and prayer could furnish. This was a special trait in the character of this great servant of God he professed a particular and

profound hatred for Satan, and this hatred he manifested on
every occasion. He, as formerly the saintly bishop of
Tours, looked upon Satan as the adversary of all that is
good, and as the constant and envenomed enemy of God
and man, whom it was one's duty on all occasions to contradict and oppose. The fine feeling of the supernatural with
which he was endowed, as well as his intimate acquaintance
with Holy Writ, made him discover the influence of the
demon in a host of things, where others did not dream of
the arch-rebel's evil presence. Thus at a time when the
number of conflagrations all over the face of France was the
theme of everybody's tongue—adapting the liturgy of the
Church—'Behold,' he said, 'the need of that prayer which
the Church on Holy Saturday, when blessing the sacred fire,
places on our lips : *From the flaming arrows of the enemy,
deliver us, O Lord.* It does not require a great deal of
ingenuity on Satan's part to bring about devastation by fire,
and when the police will seize upon the incendiary, he will
be found to be some poor wretch acting under an unaccountable impulse.'

" He was fond of quoting this passage from the great
eagle of Meaux. Satan, says Bossuet, is not only the
prince, the magistrate, the governor of this world, but, to
leave no doubt of his terrible power, St. Paul teaches us
that he is its God—*Deus hujus seculi.* In fact, he *acts the
God* upon this earth. He imitates the All-Powerful. It is
not in his power to make new creatures to oppose them to
his Master; but behold what he does. He corrupts those
of God, and turns them as far as possible against their
Author. Inflated with his success, he gets them to pay him

divine honour; he demands sacrifices; he receives vows; he has temples erected; and in all things conducts himself just like a rebel who, through envy or spite, dons the regal ornaments, and disports himself as a king. Such is the power of our enemy.

"He constantly applied to himself the warning given by the Apostle when he speaks of the enemy going about like a roaring lion : Brethren, be sober and watch ; for whilst he had the greatest faith in the watchful assistance of the guardian angels, he had no less belief in the deadly power of the evil one. The least obstacle in the way of devotion to St. Martin always gave him occasion for discussing the ruses and plans of the wicked spirit. He was entering one day the temporary chapel that was being used ; the lay-brother, the bell-ringer, and a priest were striving to open one of the doors. They had over and over attempted to turn the key in the lock, but all to no purpose ; the spring would not go back. M. Dupont came up. He was informed of what they had done or had tried to do, but seemed no way astonished at their failure. 'This is another trick of *his*,' he said, shrugging his shoulders. Then taking the key, he dipped it into the holy water fount. 'Now try,' he said. They put the key in the lock, and it turned quite freely ; and even the door opened of itself. In this instance M. Dupont did nothing more than make use of the means indicated by St. Theresa, when she declares that, according to her own experience, powerful though the demon be, a little holy water overturns all his plans and sends him hurriedly away.

"M. Dupont had a peculiar method of his own for warding off the demon, and this was both original and amusing. His principle was to humiliate the proud spirit. He thought there was not in the Scripture an expression more contemptuous or humiliating than that by which he is described in the book of Genesis *antiquus serpens, the old serpent,* because it recalls his first crime and the period of his fall; and this appellation he was never tired of reproducing."

110. *Question.*—What should "obsessed" persons do to repel the attacks of the demon?

Answer.—The answer to this question is given, more particularly because of persons that are harassed by temptations, than of persons that are obsessed; but it is useful to both.

Holy writers say, that in the first place the conscience ought to be cleared, and that we should beg of God to save us from the attacks of our enemy, by vouchsafing to us His divine help. There should be frequent confession and holy communion; for, if the devil tries to draw persons into sin, and by sin endeavours to strengthen his hold over them, so by clearing the conscience, and by frequently doing so, we meet and oppose his power. And not alone do the sacraments remove sin, but also infuse a large increase of grace into the soul.

Secondly, we ought to elicit firm and fervent acts of faith, not contenting ourselves with saying, "I believe all the Church teaches; I believe in the Roman Catholic Church," but descending to particulars, and making acts of faith in the several great dogmas of religion; and particularly in God's providence, and that He does not wish this vexation, especially if it be injurious to us either in body or soul, or if injurious to the body, that it is not useful to our soul's salvation; and that God is ever ready to send us help, and to save us. "Wherefore if we unhesitatingly trust in His goodness and His protection, there is no question but He will free us from all harassing attacks of the demon, and that under His protection we will be safe and secure" (Brognolo). There is only one reason why God permits these things to continue happening to those who put their trust in Him, and that is for their greater sanctification.

Thirdly, when these imaginary or corporeal apparitions or attacks are made upon us by the demon, then we are to call upon God for help, but especially on the holy Names of Jesus and Mary; "and the demon will have no power in that hour of hurting those who place all their confidence in God" (Brognolo). Thus trusting in the power of God, and raising our minds to Jesus and Mary, let us mock and spurn the demon's power. "Begone, Satan, in the name of God!" "What harm can you do me, when I call upon the holy Names of Jesus and Mary?" "Begone, rebellious spirit; those who trust in God have no fear of you!" And should the attacks still continue, we have but to persevere in prayer, and soon they will either wholly cease, or God will lessen their power; for, the good God permits no man to be tempted beyond his power.

Fourthly, let us show no fear of the demon's attacks. Our opponent never has so much courage as when we turn our backs and flee before him. Now, when we show cowardice before the devil, we morally turn our backs. "The devil is a fly to those who oppose him like lions. He is a lion to those who oppose him like flies" (Brognolo). "A giant if his own words are to be believed, but a pigmy if the truth were known" (*Idem*). St. Hermes was told by his angel guardian : "Do not fear the devil ; while you fear God you are the demon's master, because there is no power in him. In whom, then, there is no power, in him surely there is nothing to be feared. But He, in whom there is glorious power, He is to be feared !" And again: "The devil makes a great noise, but it is sound, and no more. Do not, therefore, fear him, and he will fly from you." And he gives a reason : "The devil has no power over those servants of God who with their whole heart believe in the Lord".

Lactantius says . "The demons can indeed injure persons, but they can injure only those who are afraid of them, and who, therefore, are not protected by the powerful and high hand of the Lord".

With regard to the power of our angel guardian, and the trust we ought to have in him, the same St. Hermes learned from his angel instructor: "Do not fear the devil; he has no power over you. I am with you, the angel of penance, and I command him; for in the Psalms it is written: He hath given his angels watch over thee, that they guard thee in all thy ways."

PART IX.

MAGIC IN OUR DAYS.

Our blessed Lord, who knew the future, said : "There shall arise false Christs and false prophets, and they shall work signs and wonders" (*Matt.* xxiv. 24).

" Signs and wonders " have been worked in our days Mesmerism, spirit-rapping, table-turning, spiritualism, are the wonders that engage men's attention to-day. And yet these are not new; they are but the re-arisen sorceries of an earlier age. Tertullian says : " Magicians work wonders; they even call up the shades of the dead. They procure children to speak with the tone of oracles; they perform preternatural things by revolving affairs; they infuse sleep; and having received the aid of angels or demons, they cause tables to divine " (*Apologia*, 23).

111. Of the sorceries of our days mesmerism is the oldest, and is therefore the first link in the chain that connects us with the witchcraft that flourished towards the close of the Middle Ages, and after they had passed away. Mesmerism is so called from its author, Franz Mesmer, a German. He was born in 1734, and studied medicine at Vienna; but, after taking out his degrees, he turned his attention to theory and experiments rather than to practice. Arguing from the relation that exists in minerals which we call magnetism, he concluded that such a connection must exist too between men. He set himself to find this connection, which he called animal magnetism; and in the year 1775 he published his theories regarding it. In the year 1782 a committee was appointed to investigate his work. He claimed that he had discovered an emanation or influence proceeding from the bodies of persons, and that this emanation had a certain action or power on the bodies of certain other persons—more powerful over some, less powerful over others; just as mind has power, less over some, more over others; or as a certain expression of face will at once interest

and (as it were) speak volumes to some parties, and will have no influence over, and be quite blank to, others. With his wonderful abilities and his patient investigations, he constructed a new system which at once engaged the learned of Europe at that day. The committee—one of whom was the celebrated Franklin—entirely reprobated the idea. They wind up their report by saying: "On blindfolding those who seemed most susceptible to the influence, all its ordinary effects were produced when nothing was done to them, but when they imagined they were magnetised; while none of its effects were produced when they were really magnetised, but imagined nothing was done. The effects actually produced were produced purely by the imagination."

Mesmer was so chagrined by the report that he retired into private life, still continued his experiments—they were his only consolation now—and died in poverty in the year 1815, being over 80 years of age.

"The mesmeric state is produced by a steady gaze at some fixed object. There is no peculiar virtue in the eyes of the mesmerist or in a metallic disc, for a spot on the wall will produce the effect. The thing requisite is a monotonous and sustained concentration of the subject's will, producing weariness and vacancy of mind; and this resembles the condition that induces reverie and sleep. No wish of the mesmeriser was ever known to affect the 'subject' until it was conveyed to him by voice or otherwise" (*Chambers' Encycl.*). "It has been clearly established that the notion of a force of any kind whatever proceeding in such cases from a person or from a magnetising apparatus is a delusion" (*Idem*).

112. *Question.*—What was the beginning and what the history of spirit-rapping ?

Answer.—The birth-place of spirit-rapping was the State of New York, and was first heard about the commencement of the year 1848. There is a village in New York State named Hydesville. A Mr. Fox and his family lived there in the above year. For some two or three months, there was heard night after night a knocking, now at the door, now at the windows—at one time on the floor, at another at the ceiling. Believing it to be some practical joke, they tried every means to discover the perpetrator—but all in vain. They grew weary of it, and wished they were done with it, but to no purpose; the knocking continued. " Wearied out by a succession of sleepless nights and of fruitless attempts to penetrate the mystery, the family had retired very early to rest, but scarcely had the mother seen the children in bed and was retiring to rest herself, when the children cried out : ' Here they are again ' Thereupon the noises became louder and more startling. Kate (one of the children, about nine years of age) remarked that as often as her father shook the windows (to know if it was they that were causing the noise) the rappings seemed to reply. Turning to where the noise was she snapped her fingers, and called out : ' Here, do as I do '. The knockings instantly responded. She called her mother : ' Only look, mother,' she said, bringing her finger and thumb together, as before. And as often as she repeated the motion (even noiselessly), the rappings answered. ' Count ten,' the mother said. Ten raps were given. ' Are you a man ?' No answer. ' Are you a spirit ?' It rapped."—*Chambers' Encycl.*

The neighbours flocked in. Questions were asked and answered. The rumour got abroad. The newspapers took it up and discussed it. A *brochure*, containing the statements of eye-witnesses, appeared in April, 1848. The invisible agents declared they were the spirits of deceased relatives and friends, and that they wished that the facts should be published. This, to a Catholic, was, or would be, evidence enough to damn them; for spirits from the other world do not return for such idle and vainglorious purposes as they seemed to seek. In Rochester, in the November of 1848, a lecture was delivered, at which it was promised the knockings would be heard. The knockings were heard, and a committee was straightway appointed to investigate. The committee failed to find any explanation of the knockings. Another was appointed on the spot. It failed. Disgusted with their failure, the assembly appointed a third. It likewise failed.

Dr. Nicolls, in a work entitled *Forty Years of American Life*, gives some of the different phases it assumed, and of the works it performed: " Dials were made with movable hands, which pointed out letters and answered questions without apparent human aid. The hands of 'mediums' without their volition wrote things beyond their knowledge. Some represented (most faithfully, it was said) the actions, voices, and appearances of persons long since dead. Others, blindfolded, drew portraits of persons they had never seen. Ponderous bodies, such as heavy dining-tables and pianofortes, were raised from the floor. Mediums were raised in the air. Writings and pictures were produced without visible hands," &c., &c.

When one rises up from reading the humble, edifying, saintly works of any one of God's great servants on this earth, and compares them with these nonsensical vagaries of invisible beings, the conclusion is at once forced on one's mind, that these things, if they be the work of supernatural agents (as undoubtedly some of them were), they can be done by no agents sent from God. They can be done by no agents sent from the solemn assembly of the departed in purgatory, and can therefore be but the works of the agents of the demon in hell.

The further history of spirit-rapping.—The report of the wonders crossed the Atlantic. In 1854 a Mrs. Haydon came over from America, but produced little or no impression. In the following year, however (1855), appeared in those islands the famous apostle of spiritualism or spirit-rapping, Mr. Daniel Dunglas Home. The manifestations which took place in his presence were of so startling a nature that all Europe was amazed—the third Napoleon opened the gates of the Tuilleries to him, and the Emperor of the Russias received him at St. Petersburg. In 1869 a committee was appointed in London to investigate the new doctrine, and many of the members of the committee that came to mock, it seems, remained to pray. The committee issued its report, and it is merely a replication of the vain, silly, aimless, unedifying, though undoubtedly wonderful, things which have been already recited.

"One of the most recent phases of spiritualism in this country," says Chambers, "is 'spirit-photographs'." Wonderful works surely! From their fruits you shall know them! Gigantic powers, angelic intelligences, debased to the poor renown of raising a weight, lifting a man in the air, moving hands or fingers that belonged to no visible body, making musical instruments play, producing paintings in pencil or colours, giving portraits of dead persons, and such silly trifling —and the agents of these nonsensical works are incensed and worshipped as deities. These be thy gods, O Israel !

113. *Question.*—Are all these the work of supernatural agents ?

Answer.—It is likely that they are not. Many of them may be attributed to sleight-of-hand, and it is wonderful what mysterious things may be done by sleight-of-hand, and to the uninitiated all but absolutely incredible things are thus performed. These, of course, are the result of natural causes ; but many, and in the case of some mediums all, are to be attributed to preternatural agents—and if to preternatural agents, it is not to God, nor the angels, nor the saints, nor even to the shades or spirits of the dead, but to the agents of the demon.

Pere Matignon writes : "All these things have frequently been accompanied by extraordinary phenomena,—apparitions of light, flames of fire, mysterious hands, phantoms visible to some of the bystanders, invisible to others, a repetition of unusual noises, mysterious knocks coming from several quarters at the same time, thunder-claps, voices which resembled those of men and sang unknown airs, harmonious sounds as if proceeding from musical instruments, sometimes even a complete concert, to which nothing was wanting except the figures of those who played or sang.

" Even in the physical order the unknown agent works wonders. He produces in some media insensibility and rigidity of limb; he will develop and enlarge bones and members of the body till they assume a monstrous proportion and shape—sometimes sudden and unexpected cures have taken place, but more frequently disturbance of mind as well as sickness of body, which, in many cases, led to insanity and suicide" (*La Question du Surnaturel*, iii., p. — c. 8).

" Now that invisible and intelligent cause (by which these things are wrought) cannot be God, nor an angel, nor a saint, but the demon. An effect always partakes of the nature of its cause. In the works wrought by the demon, neither the object, manner, medium, nor purpose, has anything dignified, useful, or holy about it. Vanity, silliness, cruelty, violence, pride, uncleanness, characterises and condemns them. Whereas to God and His angels and His saints can be attributed those works only that are in consonance with the holiness of heaven" (Bonal).

114. *Question.*—But could souls from purgatory be the cause?

Answer.—No; and for the very same reason that the angels or saints in heaven could not; for it would be all but blasphemy to assert that the angel enjoying eternal bliss would, at the command of some person on earth, not to say an unholy person, leave his home in heaven to play at silly nonsensical tricks, always to obey such a person's nod and will, and to pander to the idle curiosity of the public when ordered. In the same way it would be outrageous to assert that a soul from the ever blessed stillness and silence of the sacred prison-house of the dead—

the Christian limbo—would be brought to this life for no other purpose than to take part in vain and ridiculous antics.

115. *Question.*—Could then a soul from hell assume a spiritual body and be the cause?

Answer.—A soul that is in hell cannot leave it without God's special permission. God permits the demons to do these things, as, from the beginning of the world, He has all along permitted them to seduce men by all kinds of wiles and temptations—by assuming power, by doing extraordinary things, by pandering to men's passions—to seduce them from their allegiance to the Creator, and induce them to serve and obey the demon. But never has He permitted a soul from hell to come to earth. "Between us and them there is fixed a great chaos; so that they who would pass from hence to them cannot, nor from thence come hither" (*Luke* xvi. 26).

116. *Question.*—But perhaps they can come to testify to brethren, lest they also go to that place of torments?

Answer.—No; they cannot come. "They have Moses and the prophets, let them hear them." And assuredly if they be not permitted to come to testify to brethren, they are not permitted to come on such vain errands or for such foolish purposes as the ends and aims spirit-rapping professes and exhibits.

117. *Question.*—Is it lawful then to ask questions of those turning-tables or spirit-rappings?

Answer.—It is not lawful, even under a protest, or when

done for a joke; for if tables be turned round without any natural cause, then they can be turned by the devil only; or if knocks take place or rappings be heard without any explanatory cause, then it must be by diabolic agency; and any person holding communications with the works of the devil plainly does a forbidden thing. It would, of course, be quite a different thing if the tables were turned (as they usually are) by sleight-of-hand, and that answers were given by the same, and the whole meant for a pastime.

118. *Question.*—Is there anything wrong in being present at these *seances ?*

Answer.—If it be evident and incontrovertible that these manifestations take place by diabolic agency, then it would be wrong to assist at them. " It is not lawful," says Bonal, "to be present at those gatherings where table-turning, spirit-rapping, and question and answer take place; for, then those assisting are by their presence countenancing, and therefore participating in the sin of the promoters. Even should they go with the motive of seeing for themselves, or, more laudably still, endeavouring to refute them, it is not lawful—*we are not to do evil, that good should come out of it.*"

Where, on the other hand, it is done by sleight-of-hand, and known to be such, there can be no sin. It is however, at best, very silly and not very commendable pastime.

" Properly, therefore, has the practice of invoking the demon by table-turning, spirit-rapping, &c., and consulting him, or holding any commerce with him, been reprobated and condemned by the bishops all over the world as superstitious and damnable " (Bonal).

" In the nineteenth century, as in the most remote and illiterate ages, the human race, with its inborn curiosity for the marvellous, leaves behind it, as worthless of regard or inquiry, the only thing that is really marvellous—namely, the religion of Christ, and casts itself into the arms of superstition and devilry "'(Mons. Pie, Bishop of Pictavia).

119. *Question.*—What is meant by *clairvoyance ?*

Answer.—*Clairvoyance* is one of the effects claimed by the advocates of *animal magnetism* or *mesmerism* as the result of that connection existing between human bodies. First is the state of *sleep* brought on by the action of the magnetiser on "the subject". Second is the state of *somnambulism,* in which " the subject," while deprived of consciousness, speaks and hears, and even answers questions put to him. The third is the state of *vision* or *clairvoyance,* in which "the subject " preternaturally understands not alone his own mind and person, but likewise of others, understands sickness and its remedies, can read mysterious writing, speak in unknown languages, and can tell with accuracy and detail the most hidden or the most distant things.

120. *Question.*—What is its lawfulness ?

Answer.—Theologians as well as medical doctors differ as to whether, in the first place, such a force exists in nature, as the advocates of magnetism claim ; or whether such a questionable knowledge or power be not from the agency and influence of the demon. Some medical men hold that such a force does exist, others deny it *in toto*. Again, some would hold that as far as inducing sleep, pure and simple, by the passes of the hands, or by magnetised plates,—and even somnambulism,—such lies within the force of nature ; but, *clairvoyance* is admitted by all to be beyond its power, and is to be attributed solely to diabolic agency.

121. *Question.*—What, then, is to be our conduct on this grave question ?

Answer.—Luckily, it has been settled for us. In a pronouncement of the Sacred Congregation (28th July, 1847), the matter is thus referred to : " In case of all error being removed, all fortune-telling, and all invocation of the demon, implicit as well as explicit, the use of magnetism—*i.e.*, the merely having recourse to physical media otherwise lawful— *is not morally forbidden* (usus magnetismi, nempe merus actus adhibendi media physica aliunde licita, non est morabiter vetitus), provided also it does not lead to any immoral or wicked end. But the application of principles and media which are purely physical, to things and effects which are preternatural, and then explaining them by physical means, is nothing but a deception absolutely illicit and non-Catholic."

About *somnambulism* and *clairvoyance*, it teaches in an Encyclical to all the bishops : " When by the aid of *somnambulism* or *clairvoyance*, as they call it, women of doubtful character, and with gesticulations that can hardly be deemed modest, and who declare that they see invisible things, and who even preach sermons on religion—invoke the dead, receive responses, profess to discover distant or unknown things—when they dare to practise such and the like abominable superstitions; in all these things, no matter how the result may be produced, by art or sleight-of-hand, *while physical media are directed to performing preternatural wonders,* there is always a deception which is unlawful, contrary to the spirit of the Catholic Church, and a scandal against good morals ".

" Hence," says Bonal, "though the use of magnetism be not in every case forbidden, in no case is it allowable where the prescriptions of Christian decency be violated or infringed."

Every recurrence, therefore, to preternatural agencies for the sake of finding out secret things, or lost things, or to obtain the possession of things—by improper means—is always forbidden; as it is holding a commerce or communication with the devil.

" The soul that shall go aside after magicians and diviners, and shall commit fornication with them, I will set My face against that soul, and destroy it out of the midst of its people " (*Leviticus* xx. 6).

" If any man of the children of Israel, or of the strangers that dwell in Israel, give of his seed to the idol Moloch, dying let him die; the people of the land shall stone him, and I will set My face against him, and will cut him off from the midst of his people : and if the people of the land neglecting, and, as it were, making little of My commandment, let alone the man that hath given of his seed to Moloch and will not kill him, I will set My face against that man and his kindred, and will cut off both him and all that consented with him to commit fornication with Moloch out of the midst of their people " (*Leviticus* xx. 2, 3, 4, 5).

"A man or woman in whom there is a pythonical or divining spirit, dying let them die; they shall stone them; their blood be upon them" (*Leviticus* xx. 27).

"These two things shall come upon thee suddenly in one day, barrenness and widowhood. All things are come upon thee, because of the multitude of thy sorceries, and for the great hardness of thy enchanters. Evil shall come upon thee, and thou shalt not know the rising thereof; and calamity shall fall violently upon thee, which thou canst not keep off; misery shall come upon thee suddenly, which thou shalt not know: Stand now with thy enchanters and the multitude of thy sorceries, in which thou hast laboured from thy youth; if so be, it may profit thee anything, or if thou mayest become stronger. Thou hast failed in the multitude of thy counsels; let not the astrologers stand and save thee: they that gazed at the stars and counted the months, that from them they might tell the things that are to come to thee. Behold, they are as stubble—there is none that can save thee" (*Isaias* xlvii. 9).

"Let them come and tell us all things that are to come, and we will set our heart upon them. Show the things that are to come hereafter, and we shall know that ye are gods. Behold, you are of nothing, and your work of that which hath no being. He that hath chosen you is an abomination. I have raised up *one* from the north, and He shall come from the rising of the sun. He shall call upon My name, and He shall make princes to be as dirt, and as the potter treading clay. Behold My servant; I will uphold Him: My soul delighteth in Him. He shall not cry, nor have respect to person, neither shall His voice be heard abroad.

The bruised reed He shall not break, and the smoking flax He shall not quench " (*Isaias* xlvi. 22   .).

We now turn from these subjects of irreligion, horror, and detestation, to subjects of beauty, blessedness, and peace : (1) The state of man in the garden of Paradise, and (2) his future state in the blissful and eternal hereafter.

PART X.

THE STATE OF MAN IN THE GARDEN OF PARADISE.

122. *Question.*—What was man's state in regard to his body before his fall, and after his fall?

Answer.—Many questions are asked, says St. Bonaventure, about the first state of man; as what was the nature of his body before the fall, what of his soul, whether mortal or immortal, passible, or impassible; as also about the length of his pilgrimage here below, and the manner of his translation to the realms above : and these things, though asked about through curiosity, still may be answered not without fruit.

The first man then, he continues, according to the nature of his earthly body, was, in a manner, *immortal*, because he could ever live on without dying, but *mortal* also, after a manner, because, in certain circumstances, *he could die.* In that first state he had *the power to die*, and *the power not to die.* This, then, was the first immortality of the human body, *the power not to die.* In his second state—*i.e.*, after sin—he had *the power to die*, and no other but to die, because, in this state, *death was a necessity.* In his third state —*i.e.,* after resurrection—he shall have the power *not to die,* and *not to be able to die ;* because it belongs to that state that *death is an impossibility.* After sin, then, man's body has become *dead,* not *mortal,* as the Apostle is careful to signify —the body through sin is bad—*mortuum* not *mortale*—(*Rom.* vii. 10) ; *i.e.,* it is no longer that it has the power to die, but *it must die ;* there is a necessity upon it of dying.

St. Augustine marks the difference between the manner of living of the human body before the fall and (had it been translated to heaven without falling) of its existence there. Adam was made into *a living soul*—*i.e.,* a soul giving life to the body, but the body still standing in need of sustenance : after translation the body would have become spiritual, entirely vivified by the soul, and standing in need of no extraneous support.

The Venerable Bede says : "It is not to be believed that before the coming of sin bodies were dead, as they are now ; for thus it is the Apostle speaks : *The body by reason of sin is dead ;* but although there had not been as yet spiritual bodies, they were not at any rate *dead*—*i.e.,* such as should necessarily die ".

"Since, then," says St. Bonaventure, "the first man was both mortal and immortal in regard to his body, it may be asked whether he had the double gift from nature, or whether immortality was a privilege of grace. To which I answer, continues the Saint, *to be able to die* he had from the nature of his body ; *to be able not to die* came to him from the tree of life, and, therefore, to be reckoned as a gift of grace."

St. Augustine says : " In a certain way was man created

immortal, and this came to him from the tree of life, and not from the condition of his nature. By the condition of his animal body he was mortal; immortal by the privilege of his Creator."

From this, some think that man would have died if he had not eaten of the tree of life. There was at any rate a command given to him that he should eat of all except the tree of knowledge, and they hold he would sin by disobeying the command in the one instance, as the prohibition in the other; and that sin in either case would superinduce death. Others hold that, even though sin were not committed, by not eating of the tree of life, yet that man's power of not dying came to him from his use of the fruit of the tree; and that his abstaining from using it would of itself induce death.

"The flesh of Adam," says St. Augustine, "was thus immortal before his fall, that, strengthened by sustenance, it was free from death and free from pain, and was to continue thus immortal and thus incorruptible as long as he obeyed the commands of God. Among these commands was one that he should eat of all the fruit that was granted to him, and abstain from the one that was forbidden. By the nourishment of all these other fruits he was to preserve for his body all the privileges of immortality, until, by the natural growth of the body, he had arrived at an age, *pleasing to Almighty God; when, the human species being propagated, God would order him to eat of the tree of life. By this he would have been made perfectly immortal, and would not have stood in need of sustenance any more.*"

And again: "This also I maintain, that that tree produced such fruit as would give to the body of man everlasting existence, not after the manner of other fruit, but by some secret infusion of health ".—*Super Genesim.*

" In this passage St. Augustine appears to insinuate that by the other fruits man was to sustain his body, but from the tree of life alone was he to receive never-failing health ; from which it seems to follow that as in his own nature man found a certain mortality—*i.e.*, an aptitude to die—so also in his nature was there a certain immortality—*i.e.*, an aptitude not to die while supported by food ; but if he had stood constant the perfection of this immortality would have come to him from the tree of life " (St. Bonaventure).

After sin, however, the fruit of this tree of knowledge would not have rendered man immortal ; for thus was it decreed by God, and by Him also openly stated to man : " On whatsoever day thou shalt eat of it, thou shalt die the death " ; and again, the Holy Ghost, through St. Paul, lays down the doctrine, *The wages of sin is death,* and that doctrine is unchangeable, whether prospective or retrospective.

It is true that God said : " Lest, perhaps, he put forth his hand, and take also of the fruit of the tree of life, and live for ever " ; by *for ever* the commentators understand not an eternity but a lengthened period of existence. " *Eternum* does not mean here an endless life, but one of very long duration, and the Scripture often uses the expression in that sense ; for although the tree of life could not make man's body [after sin] immortal, it could, nevertheless, so sustain and invigorate his nature, that his body might last a very long time " (St. Bonaventure).

Our reason also would tell us that it requires no less a

power to continue a mortal body in existence for ever, than to raise a dead body to life ; now, it is only a Divine Power can raise a dead body to life, and, therefore, nothing less than a Divine Power could continue for ever a mortal body in existence. This, in another way, God told to Adam: Dust thou art, and into dust thou shalt return (*Genes.* iii.).

On the other hand, "if man had lived innocently in the garden of Paradise, fire would not have burnt him, nor water drowned him, nor want of air suffocated him, nor would any of those things which now obstruct and injure man have done him the least harm" (St. Isidore).

" The body of Adam, while in a state of innocence, could not *actually* be dissolved, although it had the power under certain conditions to be dissolved" (St. Bonaventure).

" Regarding the duration of time that they were to remain on this earth before being translated into Paradise, the Scripture lays down nothing definite. Hence it is doubtful whether, when the children were born and the justice of the human office was fulfilled (*perfectaque humani officii justitia*), the parents would be transferred to a better state, not by death but by some change ; or that the parents would remain in a certain unchangeable state, and be preserved in that state by making use of the tree of life, until their children would arrive at that state, and the number of the elect being then complete, all would be transferred at once to that better life where they were to be as the angels of God " (St. Bonaventure).

" The first men could, in the garden of Paradise, beget children, and these children would succeed to their parents, who in that case would not die, but remain in a certain fixed state, receiving vigour from the tree of life. After a time the children would arrive at the same state, until at length the number being complete, these creatures would (without passing through the gates of death) be changed into a certain quality or form in which they would be absolutely obedient to the dominion of the will, and would continue in existence without any corporal food, and by the power of the spirit alone " (St. Augustine).

There would have been no such thing as hunger or thirst; for everything would have been complied with so orderly and under such due obedience that no cravings of any kind could arise.

Answering the objection of some, that " they needed no food before sinning, because they could not be hungry unless they had sinned," St. Bonaventure says : " Hunger is truly a defect and a punishment of sin; for it is an immoderate desire of eating which man would never have felt had he not sinned; but, unquestionably, he would have sinned, if he had not taken food in order to prevent this defect. He had an appetite for food which was natural and moderate, and the suggestions of this appetite were to be obeyed in order that he should not feel the defect of hunger. It was not then a defect, but a condition of his nature, that man before his sin stood in need of food ; and in the same way it might be said that it was no defect on the part of his children, but rather a condition of their being, if, while they were still in innocence, they did not at once, instead of by slow and well-regulated steps, arrive at the fulness of their stature and the perfect mastery of their animal bodies."

In the next place it is to be seen whether, from the moment of their birth, children born in the state of innocence would enjoy the use of their senses and reason.

"Those who hold that these children would be born little, and would by slow and long intervals reach maturity, equally hold that in infancy these children would be imperfect in their knowledge and in the use of their reasoning powers, and that it is only by length of time they would arrive at the fulness of their senses and their reason" (Hugo).

"But against this some hold," he continues, "that if they did not obtain the full use of their intellect and their reason immediately after being born, there would then be a defect —ignorance, namely; and ignorance is a punishment of sin, and there would thus be a punishment of a crime before that crime was committed. But those who maintain this opinion do not sufficiently consider the word *ignorance*. There is an ignorance of things which one ought to know, and an ignorance of things which by no means come within the sphere of one's duty to know. In the first case, it would be a defect; in the latter, it would not. If such an igno-rance existed in the case of children born in a state of innocence, it would have to be attributed to a condition of their being, rather than to a defect in their nature, much less a punishment they had not yet deserved."

"Such was the state of man according to the condition of his body before his fall. From this state, however, he was to be translated, with all his posterity, to a much better and more dignified one, where he was to enjoy the celestial and eternal good prepared for him in the heavens. Man being composed of a double nature, God prepared for him a twofold gift from the beginning—one temporal, the other eternal; one visible, the other invisible; one pertaining to the body, the other to the soul; and because *that is first which is animal,* and *then that which is spiritual,* the temporal and visible gift He gave first" (St. Bonaventure).

The number of the saved is to be reckoned according to the number of the angels; but whether according to the number of the fallen or the faithful is disputed. St. Gregory says: "That heavenly city is to consist of angels and of men. Thither, we believe, as many of the human race will ascend as there are individual angels found there, in accordance with the canticle in Deuteronomy (xxxii. 8), 'He hath decreed the boundaries of peoples according to the number of the angels of God'. [This is the reading of the Septuagint. The Vulgate has: '. according to the number of the children of Israel'.]"

The more common opinion is that the number of the elect will be according to the number of the angels that fell away, inasmuch as man was destined to fill their vacant places; "so that that heavenly city would not be deprived of its proper number of citizens, nor abound with too great copiousness" (St. Bonaventure). It is reasonable also to suppose that since the angels fell from each of the nine choirs, the souls of the elect will be assumed into each of these choirs; for thus will the ruin that took place in the heavens be fully repaired. "Moreover, in this life we see that some souls are already made like to the seraphim in their use of grace, some to the cherubim, and so on; if, therefore, God gives to each according to each one's merits, it is reasonable to suppose that souls will be assumed into the different choirs; some into the choir of seraphim, some to the cherubim, and so on " (St. Bonaventure).

It may be objected that an angel is greater than a human soul, and that a certain number of souls would not at all represent an equal number of angels. St. Bonaventure answers this objection. He says: "Although an angel exceed a human soul in its natural powers—*i.e.*, comparing one creature to another; yet, if we compare them to the most Holy Trinity, whose image both angels and men are, there is no room for excellence of one above the other; nay, if any, the human nature has shown to be more exalted than the angelic nature in heaven, in its union with the divinity of the Son of God (in the first place), and in the queen-regency of the mother of God (in the second). And, granted for a moment that in natural qualities angels may exceed men, that is not a conclusive proof that they must likewise exceed them in the endowments of grace, which fall free and unfettered from the hand of God; 'the Spirit breathes where it wills'."

A Tenth Order.—St. Bonaventure discusses this question, which, to say the least, is curious, and not without interest. "Regarding these orders of angels," he says, "it may be asked whether they will stand fixed at the number *nine* or whether a *tenth* will be added."

First opinion: Some think that all men will be assumed into one or other of the nine choirs of angels; and this they consider most fitting, as representing in a triple form the three divine persons of the Blessed Trinity. According to this opinion, if the angels had never sinned, man would have still been created, and, after a certain time, translated into one or other of these heavenly choirs. *Then*, men would be meant as *companions ; now*, they are required as *repairers*. And this opinion seems to be *satis probabile*, says the Saint.

The second opinion relies on that text of St. Luke (xv. 8), where the woman having *ten* groats loses one. In this parable man is understood to be represented by the tenth drachma ; but *ten* can be used only in respect to *nine*, which is the number of the angels ; and if the tenth be found, there will, consequently, be added one order more to the nine orders of angels—that is to say a tenth, composed of men. St. Anselm seems to be of this opinion. They go on to argue that it is not fitting that men should be assumed into the choirs of angels, except those alone who in this life lived like the angels. There are the virgins who neither marry nor are given in marriage ; and hence virgins are the only ones, they say, that ought to be assumed, and from these alone are the gaps in the angelic ranks to be filled. "This position, however, cannot be accepted," says St. Bonaventure, "both because the tenth drachma represents virginal souls (men and women) as well as those that were once corrupt ; as also because many who have transgressed, and transgressed grievously (Peter and Magdalene for instance), will be preferred to many, even virginal souls, and will, without doubt, hold places superior to them."

The third and last, and (in St. Bonaventure's judgment) the most probable opinion is that, over and above the nine orders of angels a tenth shall be added, composed of those who in this life did not attain such an excellence as to entitle them to be ranked among the angels. These have been saved by the merits of Christ, and form a tenth order—

Christ, the great Sun of Justice, going back, as it were, ten degrees to reach them, in the same manner as, by the prayer of Isaias at the sick-bed of Ezechias the king, the sun returned ten degrees on the wall. "And this seems to be a very probable opinion, both on account of the imperfection of merits which many in this life only attain to, as also on account of the *perfection* of numbers which will prevail in the heavenly Jerusalem ; and the *perfection* of numbers, according to Augustine and Boethius, is not *nine* but *ten,* as we read also in the Decalogue and in decimation. And hence we can maintain that position, because it is rendered probable by the nature of cyphers, because of the finding of the tenth drachma, and because of the sun going back ten degrees" (Bonaventure). "Even the Blessed Virgin in that fatherland of ours will not be *beyond order,* and since she is far and away above all orders, she will constitute an order by herself" (*Idem*).

PART XI.

THE GLORY OF HEAVEN.

123. *Question.*—What is glory—the glory of heaven ?

Answer.—Glory is a certain excellent knowledge, combined with a certain special love. St. Thomas says : "It is clear understanding with thanksgiving". The glory of heaven, then, consists in an intimate knowledge of God, and a supernatural and all-absorbing love of Him. Hence there are as many degrees of glory in heaven as there are degrees of knowledge and of love.

Every moment of glory is an act of knowledge and of love,—a moment wherein, and an act whereby, the soul vividly knows and loves God, and all suitable things in God.

In that glory, knowledge is not foremost and love behind, nor is love quick and full and knowledge partial or wanting. No; knowledge and love go hand in hand, and are there equal.

The first and essential object of that knowledge and love is God; but in that knowledge and love of God there is an involved knowledge and love of whatever God is interested in, and whatever it is fitting the soul should know.

The names by which this glory is signified in Scripture are very touching and lovely. It is called "the eternal blessedness," "the life that knows no death," "the everlasting tabernacle," "our fatherland" (*in patria*), "an endless kingdom," "the crown awaiting the conquerors," "the paradise of God," "the inheritance," "the banquet-hall," "the bridal chamber," "sitting in the throne of Christ," "the golden Sabbath of rest".

St. Paul calls this life a "wrestling-ground," a "race-course," a "land of exile". Scholastics, on the other hand, call heaven "the comprehension of all joys," "the end of exile," "our native country".

124. *Question.*—What is the *Beatific Vision?*

Answer.—It is the clear knowledge of God by which we know Him as He is in Himself. We here know God by His works, or by being told about Him: one is the argument of natural reason, the other is the teaching of faith. A blind man could feel the heat of the sun, and could learn about it; but it is only when he would get his sight, and when he would be placed in a tropical climate, that he would know the sun as it is possible for man on our earth to know it.

The Scripture says : " This is life everlasting, that they may know Thee, the only true God, and Him whom Thou hast sent, Jesus Christ " (*John* xvii. 3).

" We know that when He shall appear we shall be like to Him, for we shall see Him as He is " (1 *John* iii. 2).

" Now we see Him as in a glass and by enigma *but then face to face.* Now I know only in part, but then [I shall know Him] as I am known " (1 *Cor.* xiii.).

To see God as He is, to know Him as He knows us— what is this but the most intimate knowledge ?

Tradition.—St. Clement, Alex. : " It is clear that no one ever during this life understood God fully ; they, however, who are clean of heart, they shall see God when they shall have attained final perfection ".

St. Augustine : " He is the invisible God, not in the eternal years, but only here below ".

St. Prosper : " In heaven there shall be such and so clear a knowledge of all things, as that even the very substance of God will be clearly and perfectly seen ".

St. Bernard : " In this shall consist eternal life, that we shall know the Father and Son, with the Holy Ghost, and that we see the triune God as He is, that is, not only as He is in us, or in other creatures, but as *He is in Himself*".

The Council of Florence defined : " The souls of the just, after death, clearly see the very God Himself, three and one, as He is ".

The Council of Vienna : " *In order to see God* the soul

needs the light of glory ". Our own reason would tell us that, if a life of grace here consists in knowing and loving God, as far as the soul and reason can, and if glory be the consummation of grace—in other words, if the next life be the complement and fulfilment of this, then that knowledge and love which were the two great virtues here must be crowned and consummated in the world to come, and therefore the fulness of knowledge and love must await those who consecrated their knowledge and love to God here; the fullest entirety being reserved for those who, with full and absolute sacrifice, made over their knowledge and love as immaculate handmaids in the service of their Creator.

Now, that knowledge is *immediate;* that is, imparted at the first glance, and without any reasoning process or delay of any kind. "To the blessed," says Pope Benedict II., "the Divine Essence shall show itself immediately, fully, clearly, and distinctly."

St. Paul says : " Everything partial (or imperfect) shall be eliminated, and everything perfect shall be there" (1 *Cor.* xiii. 12).

In this life our knowledge is partial or imperfect, for we know only by faith, and faith is a belief in the things we do not see. Such a state befits a time of trial ; but surely nothing but the full glow of knowledge becomes a time of ecstatic jubilee and joy.

The Psalmist says : " I will be filled when Thy glory shall appear" (*Ps.* xvi. 15).

It shall be also *most certain ;* that is, the mind shall have no doubt whatsoever. *But that glory shall not be equal in all.* Jovinian in the fourth century, and Luther in the sixteenth, taught that it would, thereby doing away with the merit of good works; for our glory in the next will be according to our actions in this. "Everyone shall receive his reward according to his labour" (1 *Cor.* iii. 8).

The Scripture says: "In My Father's house are many mansions" (*John* xiv. 2). St. Paul says: "The brightness of the sun is one thing, the brightness of the stars another; for star differs from star in brightness. The same way shall it be in the resurrection of the dead" (1 *Cor.* xv. 41). But it might be said it is only the *brightness of bodies* St. Paul speaks of here when he mentions the resurrection of the dead; souls do not arise from the dead; it may be the brightness of bodies. But bodies have their brightness from the souls, or, in other words, it is according to the degree of brightness of the soul that the everlasting brightness of the body will be.

The Council of Florence says: "We believe that the souls (for whom no punishment remains) will be at once received into heaven, and there clearly see God Himself as He is, *differently, however, according to the different degrees of merit, some more perfectly, some less so*".

Our own reason would tell us that greater labours and greater sacrifices and purer intentions must have more plentiful rewards. "*He that sows sparingly, sparingly also shall he reap*" (2 *Cor.* ix. 6). Again, punishment, according to the Scripture, will be of different degrees: "*The powerful shall be powerfully tormented*, and the mighty a mighty harassment pursueth" (*Wisdom* vi. 7). "As much as he hath glorified himself in pleasure, fill ye to him just such a measure of torment and woe" (*Apoc.* xviii. 7).

Finally, if all were to receive the same reward, then there would be no incitement to labour and sacrifice more than ordinarily, but, on the contrary, idleness and sloth would prevail. Therefore it is to be concluded that in heaven there are different degrees of glory.

The *Beatific Vision* excludes all idea of error: there can be no ignorance, no doubt, no error in heaven.

St. Thomas says: "The fulness of light admits of nothing erroneous".

St. Augustine says: "In that land of the blessed everything will be patent. The intellect shall suffer neither ignorance nor error; the memory neither forgetfulness nor decay."

"In and by that Vision everything partial is put away, and the desire of knowing is fully satisfied. Now this cannot be consistent with a want of due knowledge, therefore the blessed know all those things that it is opportune for them to know. In this sense it is that the Fathers use the expression, 'The blessed know all things'. *They are, however, ignorant of those things which are not necessary to the perfection of their state.*"—Bonal, *De Gratia et Gloria*, No. 362.

125. *Question.*—Is it possible for a created intellect to fully understand the infinite God?

Answer.—It is not possible. No one created can *fully* understand the essence of the Deity.

The Soul of Christ was the most blessed and the most extraordinarily endowed and adorned of all created things, and the Soul of Christ—blessed and adorable as It is, and forming even part of the Divine Person of our Blessed Lord

—does not fully understand the essence of the Deity. It does not fully understand that tremendous Word with which It is hypostatically united; and ever since the Hypostatic Union, and even now in heaven, and momentarily in the Blessed Sacrament of the Altar, the Sacred Soul of Jesus bows down and worships Its companion Divinity with all the humility and all the prostrate adoration of a creature. If, then, the ever-blessed Soul of our Divine Lord did not, does not, and never can understand *fully and truly* the infinite perfections of the Godhead, how can an ordinary soul? Neither here, then, nor in heaven can a soul (because it is finite and limited) understand fully the essence of the great God, which is, because it is God Himself, infinite, eternal, and unlimited.

" We firmly believe that God is incomprehensible," says the Fourth Lateran Council. " And truly," says Bonal, " by the comprehension of a thing is meant the understanding of that thing as it is adequate to the mind that examines it; so that, to fully comprehend a thing it is required that nothing remain hidden in that thing from the person examining it. Now, God cannot thus be understood by a created intellect; for the understanding of an infinite Being requires an intelligence adequate to it; that is to say, it also should be infinite. And, therefore, a created intellect, as being finite, is totally inadequate to understanding what is infinite. St. Paul, indeed, says: ' Thus run that you may comprehend' (1 *Cor.* ix. 24); but in this case the word *comprehension* is used in its wider and more general acceptation, that is, the attaining of what we aim at. And again he says: ' I shall know *as* I am known' (1 *Cor.* xiii. 12); he means as far as the substance and the end, but not the degree."—*De Gratia*, Nos. 361-70.

126. *Question.*—What, then, can be understood about God?

Answer.—The blessed in heaven, as far as it is possible, and as far as their merits deserve, see the Divine Essence in the Trinity of Persons.

The Scripture says : "We will see God as He is" (1 *John* iii. 2). If we see God as He is, and if God be Father, Son, and Holy Ghost, then we must see the Three Divine Persons. And St. John says "that our company be with the Father and with His Son, Jesus Christ" (1 *John* i. 3) ; and if our company be with the Father and the Son, then our company must be with the Holy Ghost, for Father and Son can be in no place from which the Holy Ghost is excluded. Even when we receive Holy Communion, we receive, with the Divinity of Jesus, the Father and the Holy Ghost ; for, as theology teaches, God the Son can be nowhere but God the Father and God the Holy Ghost must be there also.

And from the decision of the Council of Florence, which says : "We define that their souls see clearly God Himself, *Three and One*, as He is," there is no longer any room left to question it.

Our own reason would tell us, that to Each of the Three Divine Persons we owe a special gratitude, because from Each of the Three we have received special graces and favours ; and, therefore, heaven would have something wanting to it if One of these Three Divine Persons were absent, or that we did not see Him as intimately as the other Persons of the Sacred Trinity. Moreover, in this life we believe in the Three Divine Persons; that is an article of our faith. In the next life comes the clear and full enlightenment of all we believed in this. The Trinity is one of those mysteries of belief; shall It remain absolutely clouded from us, and shall we know no more about it for all eternity in heaven than we do here on earth? That is not like the good God, nor like what we feel in our souls, nor is it what theology teaches.

127. *Question.*—Shall the blessed know about other creatures—friends on earth, &c.?

Answer.—Yes. Perfect happiness means that nothing shall be wanting whose presence would ensure that happiness. Now, the knowledge of certain things would undoubtedly secure, if not increase, that happiness; and, therefore, the knowledge that would perfect the happiness of their state shall not be wanting. They shall, therefore, know—

(1) All objects of natural science on this earth, and all its order and beauty and conservation, the planets, the heavenly bodies, their substance, movements, laws—so that an infant, who has been but a moment baptised and dies, will know more in the instant after its death than all the professors of all the sciences on this earth.

St. Augustine says: "The angels, and therefore all others (in heaven), without doubt know the universal creation in the Person of the Word".

This is a thirst in our nature—an instinct planted there by God—to search after, and, if possible, to understand all things; and this thirst can be satiated only in heaven.

(2) They shall know all the mysteries of faith that they believed in here on earth.

St. Augustine says : " What shall we see ? What but the great God and all those things which we now believe, although we do not see."

And justly, because the seeing them in heaven is the reward of our believing them on earth.

(3) The blessed shall know in heaven all those they knew on this earth. Every pleasure or enjoyment that is innocent and lawful here shall be perpetuated in the realms beyond the sky. The friendship of friends, the affections of parents or relatives, the innocent society of companions—all these shall live in the world to come ; and we shall be happier there in the friendship of friends, for there shall be no mistake and no deceit there; and we shall rejoice in the affections of parents or relatives, when these shall be purged of all that is empty or vain, or disagreeable or selfish ; and we shall be delighted in the society of companions, when nothing trivial shall engage our thoughts, and no misunderstanding shall arise, for sin and sorrow are long since wiped from the heart.

" For a nobler state are we destined," says Tertullian. " We shall arise, and enter a spiritual society, where we shall know our friends as fully as we do ourselves." " Oh ! what a blessed meeting," cries out St. Cyprian, " when there on that shore a multitude shall await us—a multitude of those we knew and loved ! And our eyes shall see one another, and our hearts shall beat with gladness, and the whole of that crowd shall be suffused with one common joy."—*De Immortalitate.*

To know one another! Oh, if we could but know one another here, we should have more patience than we have with one another. We should then judge no one rashly; we should make allowances and excuses for them, as we do for ourselves. We should even see how innocent in their hearts they are, those whom perhaps we bitterly blame. Earth were more like a heaven did we know one another.

(4) And not alone in heaven, the blessed will also see the friends they left on this earth. The little sister that went in the early days, with the blue and white dress, and the flaxen locks—from heaven she looks down, and prays for the little brother or sister that played with her in the summer days long ago. The lonesome eyes and the breaking heart (and whose is like to hers?), the poor dying mother, and the little children peeping in at the door, or stealing round her bed, and they bidden to be silent—the lonesome eyes close and the broken heart is still, but from heaven that loving mother still looks down on her little children, and guards them with all the old wistful longing and affection.

St. Gregory says: "Our brethren that are gone before us, do they not see those who are still in danger, and do they not tremble with anxiety? Or, are they who know God all in all, and who drink of Him who is all charity, so devoid of charity as not to remember them?"

"For although," says St. Cyprian, "they be sure of their own happiness, still they are full of anxiety for ours."

And the Council of Sens says: "For the blessed the Divinity is a continual and faithful mirror, in which there is shown to them whatever could interest them".

(5) "The blessed do not know all things absolutely, the

present, the future, or what is possible ; for to know all these has nothing to do with their happiness, nor is it anywhere mentioned in the Scriptures that they have such knowledge granted them. Nay, regarding even the day of judgment, Christ expressly denies that they know it. " But of that day and hour no one knoweth, not even the angels of heaven " (*Matt.* xxiv. 36). " According to several, they do not know the thoughts of men's hearts " (Bonal). They know, however, our thoughts when we turn to them and beg their intercession.

128. *Question.*—What means have they of knowing about all these things ?

Answer.—Here on earth we have various means of knowing about things. If things are present, we see them. If our friends are present, we speak to them, we hear them. If they are absent, they write to us or telegraph to us, or we learn about them from other persons, or from the public papers, and so on. That is the way we on earth know ; but in heaven how do they know ? It is hard to explain. It is easy to answer and say, " They know all these things in the Beatific Vision ". That is true ; but how, in what way, or what does that mean ? With our limited knowledge, and our dependence on sensible signs, it is difficult for us to comprehend it. We may say, as men see a thing in a glass, so the blessed see in God all things that He wishes them to see. Or again, as in dreams we sometimes understand certain appearances or signs to signify certain things—we ask ourselves, when we awake, why, and cannot tell—so, if we might thus express it, by that dream-like spiritual alphabet, but in a sense immensely more dignified and distinct, the blessed understand rather than see things in God. It is almost wasting time trying to explain; the man blind from his birth has as much idea of the colours of the rainbow, the child deaf and dumb has as much notion of the lapping of the waves on the seashore, the singing of the birds, the laughter of the children, the sighing of the evening gales, or the music of the wind-played harp, as we could conceive of the Beatific Vision; for human eye never saw, and human ear never heard, and human heart never conceived the rapturous things God has in store for those that love Him.

129. *Question.*—What shall be the love of the blessed for God?

Answer.—It is *de fide* that in heaven we shall love God fully and perfectly.

"God is charity, and who remaineth in charity remaineth in God, and God remaineth in him" (1 *John* iv. 16). "Of the torrent of Thy delight shalt Thou fill them. I will be satisfied when the glory of the Lord shall appear" (*Ps.* xvi. 15).

The blessed, therefore, seeing God, shall love Him fully and perfectly, and He shall so overwhelm them with the fulness of His love, as with a torrent of delights, that their hearts shall be filled and they shall have no desire for more. In this matter we may expect the highest and most glowing oratory of the Fathers. Nor are we mistaken.

St. Augustine says: "How great shall that happiness be where no evil shall come and no good shall be denied!

Life shall be given up to one thing, the praises of God, who shall be all in all to the Blessed. He will be the object of all their desires, who will be beheld without faith's obscurity; He shall be loved without satiety, and hallowed without weariness."

St. Bernard : "If faith and hope so initiated them that in this land of exile they were called children of God, without doubt knowledge and love shall perfect them once they enter their Father's home ".

Our own reason would tell us that the child, after its wanderings, on its return to its parent, will be received with all the warmth and hospitality that the father can command, especially if, during the darksome and weary years of its absence, that child had been all along engaged about "his Father's business ". We may make a guess, then, at heaven. A poor man will have but a poor feast, common fare, plain furniture, when his child returns. A rich man will have rich apartments, a rich banquet, rich furniture, wine, and lights, and attendants. A nobleman will have something still more elegant, and a king will welcome back his child in sumptuous, regal style. But the King of heaven—how will He act? Will He hide away and grudge the riches of His kingdom to His children? Will no new garments be ordered, and no ring put on their fingers?— the garments that typify the beautiful knowledge, the clothing of the soul; the ring, the torrent of His love? These are the riches of the heavenly kingdom—knowledge and love ; and these in abundance the good God shall pour out on each child of His that was lost and is found, dead and come to life again.

130. *Question.*—Will this love be equal in all?

Answer.—No; it will be unequal; some of the blessed being more inundated with the torrent of God's love than others, just as. some will be more illuminated with knowledge than others. And the reason of both is because some have merited more, some less, during their term of probation on this earth of ours. But, as has been said, knowledge and love will in themselves be equal in the same person.

131. *Question.*—What is one blessed effect of this knowledge and love?

Answer.—That we shall never sin again. Illuminated with this knowledge, and inundated with this love, the soul will never feel a desire for anything else but to praise, love, and enjoy God. It is a question between the two great mediæval schools of theologians—the Dominicans and Franciscans, or, as they are known to the student of theology, the Thomists and the Scotists—whether that impossibility does arise intrinsically from the Beatific Vision; *i.e.*, that the Beatific Vision by its illumination would remove all ignorance from the intellect, and by its charity would possess the heart *so absolutely* that sin could not be even thought of— that is the opinion of the former; or, as the Scotists teach, that even though the Beatific Vision illuminated the intellect and inundated the heart, that still the blessed may sin, and that therefore there is furthermore required a special assistance of God's goodness. There are beautiful arguments in favour of both sides, equally honourable to God and equally consoling to man. For ourselves, it is enough to know that

God uses no coercion with the blessed to prevent them from sinning. If coercion were there, heaven would not be heaven. There is coercion in hell. The demons and the damned can never leave it. They are not at option even to turn to God, for God will not give them the grace. In heaven it is different. Absolutely speaking, the blessed are at option to turn from God. So much does God even still desire to pay homage to human liberty, and so much does He desire to be served by none but willing hands. That, however, never will be. To-morrow's sun may not rise, the young offspring may refuse the mother's nursing, the trees may refuse to raise their leafy tops to heaven, the rivers may turn inland and forget to run towards the ocean, the needle may not answer to the magnet. All these things may be: when will they be? Sooner than the blessed in heaven shall turn away from God.

132. *Question.*—Is God a liberal rewarder?

Answer.—In Genesis xxii. we read that God ordered Abraham to sacrifice to Him his only son, Isaac. He was the child of promise and the son of the patriarch's old age. Yet he did not hesitate. And when he had his hand stretched forth to obey God's command, God said to him, " Do it not ". But because Abraham had shown his readiness to obey Him, God said : " By My own Self have I sworn, because thou hast done this thing.　　　I will bless thee, and I will multiply thy seed as the stars of heaven, and as the sand that is by the sea-shore　　　and in thy seed shall be blessed all the nations of the earth, because thou hast obeyed My voice."

In the second book of Kings (vii.) we read that King David, in his own mind, was comparing his beautiful palace with the poor tent in which was lodged the Ark of the Lord, and he resolved with himself to erect a house and temple for the Ark. He merely resolved to do so. He did not do it. Yet the Bible tells us God rewarded him. " But it came to pass that night that the word of the Lord came to Nathan the prophet, saying: Go and say to My servant David   The Lord will make thee a house. And when thy days shall be fulfilled, and thou shalt sleep with thy fathers, I will raise up thy seed after thee   and I will establish the throne of his kingdom for ever."

What God will give us is a kingdom in the world to come. What wonderful sacrifices men have made to reach a kingdom on earth! Those even are accounted happy that have amassed wealth for themselves. But where is the monarch that will bestow a kingdom on us? And if a king gave a kingdom to his servant, the reward would be counted exceeding great. But what is an earthly to a heavenly kingdom? What is one year, one moment, one second, to millions of millions of years! And then what the uneasiness, uncertainty, trouble, anxiety of the earthly kingdom compared to the unchangeable, unalloyed, tranquil bliss of the eternal one? God is, then, a most liberal Rewarder!

133. *Question.*—Is there any difference between *Grace* and *Glory?*

Answer.—These terms are here taken in their usual signification. The soul is clothed in *Grace* here, in *Glory* hereafter. The one is but the commencement of the other.

God, by baptism, has made us His own children, and heirs of the kingdom of heaven; and just as parents will put infants' dress on their children, and by and by will clothe them in men's attire, so God clothes the soul, while it is here, in *Grace*, which is, as it were, the children's suit, compared to the beautiful vesture of *Glory* that is awaiting its maturity in the land beyond the skies. Hence it happens that when a man puts off by mortal sin the raiment of *Grace* here, he at the same time puts away from him the complement vesture of *Glory* that was awaiting him in heaven.

"For we know that if our earthly house of this habitation be dissolved, that we have a building of God, a house not made with hands, eternal in heaven. For in this also we groan, desiring to be clothed with our habitation which is from Heaven, yet so that we may be found clothed, not naked. For we also who are in this tabernacle do groan, being burdened; because we would not be unclothed, but clothed over, that what is mortal may be swallowed up by life" (2. *Cor.* v. 1-4).

"Grace is a participation in the nature and life of the Divinity; so that faith and charity are a participation even in that divine act whereby the Father begets the Son, and from Father and Son the Holy Ghost eternally proceeds. Wherefore, nothing can be thought of more incomparably excellent than a participation in that life, in which the very essence of the Deity consists."—Bonal.

"Grace and glory are both referred to the same class, for grace is nothing else than the commencement of glory in us."—St. Thomas.

Grace is the highest perfection of man here, glory is his ultimate perfection hereafter.

Bossuet says: "The life of grace and the life of glory is *the same*, and there is no more difference between the one and the other than between childhood and mature manhood. In *glory*, life is consummated; here below it is but growing; yet is it the same life. Like the pearl, hidden and concealed, is our life in this world; like it shining in its brilliancy, studded and enchased, is our life in the next."—*Sermon on the Feast of All Saints.*

134. *Question.*—What, then, are the special effects of *Glory?*

Answer.—Its effects are threefold: (1) It elevates the created intellect, and makes it not alone angelic in its insight and perception, but even God-like. (2) It disposes the intellect—it gives the intellect strength to receive and support the unveiled, unshadowed vision of the Deity. We put up our hands before our eyes when we look at the sun. The eagle looks at it directly. Moses could not see God and live. The Israelites could not even bear to look on the face of Moses, their fellow-man. Our intellect could not bear to see the full glory of God. Nor, again, would our weak love stand the strain. People have died of an unexpected joy. So with us; our souls could not bear the sweetness and richness of that torrent of delights—God's love in heaven. It therefore disposes the intellect. And (3) after disposing it to do so, then it elicits or produces in our created intellect, and by our created intellect, an act participating in the essential acts (as above said) of the

Deity. So that, being now installed as the children of God, we (with our tremendously elevated and strengthened intellects) do as we see our Father doing.

135. *Question.*—Do the souls, then, who, on leaving this world, have by penance or indulgences wiped away all punishment due to sin, enter immediately into heaven ?

Answer.—Instantaneously. "It is easy before God *in the day of death* to reward everyone according to his ways" (*Ecclesiasticus* xi. 23).

Tradition.—Council of Florence says : "We believe that the souls of those who, after baptism, have incurred no stain whatsoever of sin, as well as of those who have washed away the stains of their sins, will be received into eternal glory, and there behold face to face the very God Himself, Three and One, as He is".

It is not here said that there shall be delay. Nor is there any reason to suppose there shall be delay ; for if no delay and no respite is given to a soul condemned to hell, but is hurried off at once, surely it would be saying that God was more prone to punishing than to rewarding if a soul were, on the other hand, detained from entering immediately into glory.

Apart from that, God's history with man has been one long unbroken series of anxiety and eagerness and desire to have man near Him. He came down to him in the twilight shades of Eden ; He died for him on the Cross ; He lives for him in the Blessed Sacrament ; His delight is to be with the children of men. Will He then delay, when an opportunity offers, and no decree stays His hand—will He delay to take the human soul that He has so yearned after to the realms of joyful bliss, where He and the soul—if we might reverently say it—will live in a happy and blessed union for ever? The very moment then the soul leaves the body, if there be no penalty to be paid, no stain to be washed away, that moment the soul enters the glory of God.

136. *Question.*—Did anyone while here on this earth enjoy the Beatific Vision?

Answer.—Yes; the Soul of our Divine Lord, from the first moment of Its young life in the sacred womb of His Virgin Mother, and all along during Its life on earth, enjoyed it.

Of our Blessed Lady, Suarez says that it may be piously and probably believed that this singular grace was at times conceded to her.

Of all other men, no one has ever seen God face to face. Of Moses and St. Paul it is doubtful. God Himself said to Moses: "You cannot see My face; for man may not see Me and live". And St. Paul says that he was rapt indeed to the third heavens; and he tells us for what, that he would hear secret words, but not that he would see God (*ut audiret verba arcana*).

PART XII.

THE GLORY OF THE BODY.

137. *Question.*—What shall be the glory of the body?

Answer.—In heaven there are two sorts of glory: one,

belonging to the soul, comprising knowledge and love, and therefore called *essential ;* the other, belonging to the body, and called *accidental.* This comprises the privileges with which God will clothe our mortality.

138. Of the body, St. Anselm reckons seven most excellent and glorious qualities : beauty, agility, fortitude, penetrability, health, pleasure, and perpetuity.

Of *beauty,* or, as we shall better understand it, perfection of body, our Blessed Lord says that the bodies of " the just shall shine as the sun in the kingdom of their Father " (*Matt.* xiii.). Here below there are many diseases and many deformities. But in the kingdom of heaven there shall be none blind, lame, or defective ; but such defects shall remain as would redound to the glory of the elect. For this reason our Blessed Lord retains His five Sacred Wounds ; for this reason also the martyrs' bodies shall have their scars, but these scars shall shine with an especial and transcendent glory, on account of their being borne for Christ.

The second quality shall be *agility.* We know what is matter ; we know it by its dull, lazy cloddishness. Spirit is totally opposed to matter. Our souls and our bodies are of diverse substances. In this sense our soul is agile, our body is not. A bird winging its rapid flight is agile. Lightning is agile : a ray of light can travel about 12,000,000 of miles in a minute. Our memory is agile : it can, in a second, speed to the farthest distance, or recollect the most remote occurrence. Our bodies, then, will become spiritualised after their resurrection. The Sacred Body of our

Divine Saviour by this quality ascended into heaven after His Resurrection ; and by this quality also shall our bodies, more rapid than lightning, quicker than thought, rise from the dead, and ascend on high, when our mortality puts on immortality. " Neither did Christ ascend into heaven solely by virtue of His power as God, but also by the power which he possessed as man " (*Cat. Council. Trent*). But in hell they shall not be able to move hand nor foot. The third is fortitude or strength. St. Anselm says that a glorified body will be so endowed with strength that it could move the whole earth. Of St. Peter of Alcantara, the great Franciscan Father that practised such heroic mortifications and penances, and of whom St. Theresa tells that God told her anything she would ask for through his intercession would be granted, of him it is told that one day falling into an ecstasy of love he grasped the tree beside which he was standing, drew it from its roots, and bore it with him into the air. Such the power of the love of God even here on earth.

The fourth is penetrability. This will be understood from an instance in the life of our Blessed Lord after His Resurrection. The Apostles were gathered together in a room. The doors were carefully fastened, for the crowd outside in the streets of the city talked of the men that followed the Nazarene, and the Apostles were alarmed and afraid. All at once, without a door being open, a figure stood in their midst. Then they became frightened. Before they had time to recognise Him they perhaps began to say in their own minds : " How did He get in ? If others get in in the same way, what will become of us ?

We are no longer safe even here!" And, answering their thoughts, our Blessed Lord said: "Fear not. It is I." Here a corporal body, of the same flesh and blood as ours,—the only difference being that it was glorified,—passed through other substances, *and passed through them by its natural privilege as a glorified body.* After resurrection the same privilege shall belong to our bodies.

The fifth quality is health. By health we understand absence of sickness or pain in the first place, and, in the next, each several member and joint and part performing easily and agreeably its appointed function or task. Now, in heaven there shall be no pain, no discomfort, no uneasiness.

Sometimes pain of the body arises from anguish of the mind; "but in heaven there shall be death no more, nor mourning, nor crying, nor sorrow shall be any more, for the former things are passed away; and He that sat on the throne said: 'Behold I make all things new'."—*Apoc.* xxi. 4, 5.

St. Liguori says: "In that place of bliss there are no sorrows, no infirmities, no poverty, no inconveniences, no vicissitudes of day or night, of cold or of heat. In that kingdom there is a continual day, always serene; a continual spring, always blooming. In Paradise there are no persecutions, no envy, for all love each other with tenderness, and each rejoices at the happiness of the others, as if it were his own."

The sixth perfection or privilege is delight. Each sense of man shall be delighted with an exceeding and special delectation peculiar to itself, and rejoicing it beyond worlds of happiness.

St. Anselm says : " All the whole glorified body will be filled with abundance of all kind of comfort—[this very body that presently we have]—the eyes, the ears, the nose, the mouth, the hands, the throat, the lungs, the heart, the stomach, the back, the bones, the marrow, every part shall be replenished with such unspeakable sweetness and pleasure, that truly it may be said that the whole man is made to drink of the river of God's divine delights, and made drunk with the abundance of God's house ". Oh! how careful ought I to be over the senses and members of my body, and how immaculately ought I endeavour to preserve them, if these members of my body are going to be with God's angels before God's throne in heaven! And they are, please God, going to be there.

St. Liguori says : " Perhaps we imagine that the beauty of heaven resembles that of a wide extended plain covered with the verdure of spring, interspersed with trees in full bloom, and abounding in birds fluttering about and singing on every side ; or that it is like the beauty of a garden full of fruits and flowers, and surrounded by fountains in continual play. *Oh ! what a Paradise* to behold such a plain or such a garden ! But, oh ! how much greater are the beauties of heaven ! "

St. Bernard cries out : " O man ! if you wish to understand the blessings of heaven, know that in that happy country there is nothing which can be disagreeable, but everything that you can desire ".

Speaking of the sense of sight, St. Liguori again says: "The sight shall be satiated with beholding the beauty of that city. How delightful to behold a city in which the streets should

be of crystal, the houses of silver, the windows of gold, and
all adorned with the most beautiful flowers ! But, oh ! how
much more beautiful shall be the city of Paradise ! The
beauty of the place shall be heightened by the beauty of the
inhabitants.   St. Theresa once saw one of the hands of
Jesus Christ, and was struck with astonishment at such
beauty."

Of all our senses the sense of smell is the keenest : the
most easily offended, as it is the most quickly delighted.
We know the beautiful scent of hay and corn when
rambling through the country-side in the golden autumn.
We know the scent of flowers.   Travellers tell us of isles in
the ocean that have earned for themselves the distinctive
title of "aromatic".   For miles before the ship comes
within reach of them the sailors perceive the scent ; for
miles after passing the beautiful odour is wafted along the
seas.   Oh, how sweet its breath must be !

> " The gale that sighs along
> Beds of oriental flowers."

In heaven, says St. Liguori, " the sense of smell shall be
satiated with odours, but with the odours of heaven ".

" The hearing," says he, " shall be satiated with the
harmony of celestial choirs.   St. Francis once heard, *for a
moment*, an angel playing on a violin, *and he almost died
through joy.*   How delightful must it be to hear the saints
and angels singing the divine praises ! ' They shall praise
Thee for ever and ever ' (*Ps.* lxxx. 3)   In a word,
there are in Paradise all the delights which man can desire."

St. Augustine says : " Were God to show His face to the
damned, hell would be instantly changed into a paradise of

delights"; and he adds: "Were a departed soul allowed the choice of *seeing God and suffering the pains of hell*, or, *of being freed from those pains, but deprived of the sight of God, it would prefer to see God and to endure those torments*".

The *seventh priviege* of a glorified body is called perpetuity. "The just shall live for ever" (*Wisdom* v.). When our first parents were in the garden of Eden, they were to eat of a tree called *the Tree of Life*, and the fruit of that tree kept away sickness, disease, accidents, old age, decay, death. While a person ate of that tree none of those things could happen to him. A glorified body does not stand in need of eating at all. Nothing could harm it. No contagion could bring it sickness; no accidents could cause it injury; no number of years could induce old age or decay; no enemies, no sword, no poison, could bring it death, or even do it the slightest harm: it is absolutely invulnerable to all.

"And this is one of the chief prerogatives and most excellent dignities of a glorified body," writes an English Jesuit of the penal days, "whereby all care, doubt, and fear, all danger of hurt and annoyance is taken away. *For if all the world should fall together on such a body it could not hurt nor harm it anything at all*."—*Parson's Christian Directory.*

Summing up all, St. Liguori says: "In beholding the beauty of God, the soul shall be so inflamed and so inebriated with divine love, that she shall remain happily lost in God; for she shall entirely forget herself, and for all eternity shall think only of loving and praising the immense good which she shall possess for ever, without the fear of having it in her power ever to lose it. In this life holy souls love God ; but they cannot love Him with all their strength, nor can they always actually love Him." St. Thomas teaches that "this perfect love is only given to the citizens of heaven ; they alone love God with their whole hearts, and never cease to love Him actually".

139. The ancient chronicles tell a beautiful story illustrative of the happiness of heaven, which Longfellow has thus put in verse, in his own tender Catholic way :

> " One morning, all alone,
> Out of his convent of grey stone,
> Into the forest, older, darker, greyer,
> His lips moving as if in prayer,
> His head sunken upon his breast,
> As in a dream of rest,
> Walked the monk Felix ".

The summer dawn, the woodlands, and the beautiful forest trees are described.

The old monk was reading St. Augustine's work, *The City of God* (*de Civitate Dei*), but could not understand it. " I believe, O God, what herein I have read ; but, alas ! I do not understand."

> " And, lo ! he heard
> The singing of a bird,
> A snow-white bird, that from a cloud
> Dropped down,
> And among the branches brown
> Sat singing
> So sweet, and clear, and loud,
> It seemed a thousand harp-strings ringing.
> And the monk Felix closed his book,
> And long, long,
> With rapturous look,

He listened to the song,
And hardly breathed or stirred,
Until he saw, as in a vision,
The land Elysian,
And in the heavenly city heard
Angelic feet
Fall on the golden flagging of the street."

Suddenly he wakes from his reverie, and hears his own convent bell ringing—the convent that he thought he had left but that morning.

"And he retraced
His pathway homeward, sadly and in haste."

But there was a change in the convent, a change in all things; he knew not a face in the convent.

"'A stranger, and alone
Among that brotherhood,
The monk Felix stood.
'Forty years,' said a friar,
'Have I been Prior
Of this convent in the wood,
But for that space
Never have I beheld thy face!'

"The heart of the monk Felix fell;
And he answered, with submissive tone:
'This morning, after the hour of Prime,
I left my cell;
And wandered forth alone,
Listening all the time
To the melodious singing
Of a beautiful white bird,
Until I heard
The bells of the convent ringing
Noon from their noisy towers.
It was as if I dreamed;

For what to me had seemed
Moments only had been hours ! '

" ' Years ! ' said a voice close by.
It was an aged monk who spoke,
From a bench of oak
Fastened against the wall ;—
He was the oldest monk of all.
For a whole century
Had he been there,
Serving God in prayer,
The meekest and humblest of His creatures.
He remembered well the features
Of Felix ; and he said—
Speaking distinct and slow :
' One hundred years ago,
When I was a novice in this place,
There was here a monk, full of God's grace,
Who bore the name
Of Felix, and this man must be the same '.

        " And straightway
They brought forth to the light of day
A volume old and brown,
A huge tome, bound
In brass and wild boar's hide,
Wherein were written down
The names of all who had died
In the convent, since it was edified.
And there they found,
Just as the old monk had said,
That on a certain day and date,
One hundred years before,
Had gone forth from the convent-gate
The monk Felix, and never more
Had entered that sacred door.
He had been counted among the dead,
And they knew, at last,
That, such had been the power

Of that celestial and immortal song,
A hundred years had passed,
And had not seemed so long
As a single hour."
—*The Golden Legend.*

140. *A Comparison.*—"Some divines use a consideration of the three places whereunto man by his creation is ordained. The first of these places is our mother's womb; the second, this present world; the third, '*cœlum empyreum*,' the place of bliss in the life to come. In what proportion or measure the second does exceed the first, in a much greater does the third exceed the second; so that as far as the world does surpass the womb of one woman, so much, in all beauty, delights, and majesty, does the place of heavenly bliss surpass all this whole world with the ornaments thereof. And as much as a man living in the world does exceed an infant before it is born for strength of body, beauty, wit, understanding, learning, and knowledge, so much, and far more, does a saint in heaven surpass all men in this world. The nine months also of life in the mother's womb are not so little in respect of any man's age in the world, as is the longest life on earth in respect of everlasting life in heaven."—*Parson's Directory.*

St. Augustine says: " O, my Lord ! if Thou for this vile body of ours hast given us so great and innumerable benefits, from the firmament, from the air, from the earth, from the sea, by light, by darkness, by heat, by shadows, by dews, by showers, by winds, by rain, by birds, by fish, by beasts, by trees, by multitudes of herbs and variety of plants, and by the ministry of all Thy creatures, O sweet Lord ! *what manner of things*, how great, how good, and how innumerable are those which Thou hast prepared for us in Thy heavenly country, where we shall see Thee face to face ! If Thou do such great things for us in *our prison*, what wilt Thou give us *in our palace ?* If Thou givest so many things in this world both to good and evil men, what hast Thou laid up for good men in the world to come ? If both Thy enemies and Thy friends *are well provided for in this life,* what will Thy friends receive *in the life to come ?* If there be so great solace *in these days of tears,* what joy will there be in that day of the marriage ? If our jail or prison contain so great matters, what will our country and kingdom do ? O my Lord and God, Thou art a great God ! And great is the multitude of Thy magnificence and sweetness ! And as there is no end of Thy greatness, nor number of Thy mercies, nor depth of Thy wisdom, nor measure of Thy benignity, so is *there neither end, number, limit, nor measure of Thy rewards to them that love Thee and do fight for Thee".* —*Lolil.,* c. xxi.

When God establishes an everlasting home for Himself and for His elect, and when He that is infinite all but exhausts the infinite treasures of His omnipotence on the wealth and beauty of that home, what must it be like ? St. John the Evangelist says that " *the whole place* will be *of purest gold ;* that *the wall* going around the city shall be all of a precious stone called *jaspis.* This wall has *twelve gates* of twelve rich stones, *called margarites,* and every gate an entire margarite. *The streets* of the city are paved with *gold, interlaid with pearls and precious stones.* The light of the city is the clearness and splendour of Christ Himself— shining brighter than a thousand suns—who sits in the midst thereof. *There was no night in that city, nor did any defiled thing enter thereunto : but they who are within,"* says he, "shall reign for ever and ever " (*Apoc.*).

Cardinal Hugo says : " In this vision of God we shall know, we shall love, we shall rejoice, we shall praise. We shall know the very secrets and judgments of God, which are a depth without bottom ; as also the causes, natures, beginnings, issues, and ends of all creatures. *We shall love incomparably both God, for the infinite causes of love that we see in Him, and our brethren and companions,* as much as ourselves, for that we shall see them as much loved by God as ourselves, and for the same cause for which we are loved. Whence ensues that our joy will be without measure, both because we shall have a particular joy for everything we love in God, which things are infinite, and also for that we shall rejoice at the felicity of every one of our brethren as much as at our own ; and by that means we shall have as many distinct felicities as we shall have distinct companions in our felicity, who being without number, it is no wonder that Christ said : ' Enter thou into the joy of thy Lord,' and not : ' Let thy Lord's joy enter into thee,' because no created heart can receive the fulness and greatness of this joy. And hereof finally it does ensue that we shall praise God without end or weariness, with all our heart, with all our strength, with all our powers, with all our parts, according to what the Scripture says : ' Happy are they that live in Thy house, O Lord, for they will praise Thee for ever and ever '."

141. Our Saviour, in the Gospel, said : " Blessed are the

17*b*

clean of heart, *for they shall see God"*. *To see God.* This then is a reward. It must be a very great reward, when it is promised to those who are especially dear to God on this earth—*the clean of heart.*

St. Augustine says : " There is a sight and a vision which of itself is sufficient to make a man happy and blessed for ever—a vision which neither eye has seen in this world, nor ear has heard, nor heart conceived—a vision that surpasses all the beauty of earthly things. We shall see God face to face. We shall see and know the power of the Father, the wisdom of the Son, the goodness of the Holy Ghost. We shall know the indivisible nature of the blessed Trinity. The sight of God is the full beatitude, the total glorification of men and angels ; to see and behold Him that made both heaven and earth ; to see and behold Him that made us and will glorify us. O joy above all joys ! and without which there is no joy, when shall I enjoy Thee, to see my God that dwells in Thee. O peace of God that passes all understanding, wherein the souls of the saints do rest with Thee, O Lord ; and everlasting joy is upon their heads, and joy and exultation is theirs, and all pain is fled from them. O Lord, in this kingdom of Thine there is infinite joy without sadness ; health without sorrow ; life without labour ; light without darkness ; felicity without abatement ; all good without evil. Here youth flourishes that never grows old ; life that knows no end ; beauty that never fades ; love that never cools ; health that never diminishes ; joy that never ceases. Here sorrow is never felt ; complaint is never heard ; sadness never experienced ; nor evil success ever feared, *because they possess Thee, O Lord, who art the perfection of their felicity.*"

142. *Exhortation of St. Liguori.*—" Let us then, brethren, courageously resolve to bear patiently with all the sufferings which shall come upon us during the remaining days of our lives : to secure heaven they are little or nothing. Rejoice then ; for all these pains, sorrows, and persecutions shall, if we be saved, be to us a source of never-ending joys and delights. 'Your sorrow shall be turned into joy' (*John* xvi. 20). When, then, the crosses of this life afflict us, let us raise our eyes to heaven, and console ourselves with the hope of Paradise. At the end of her life, St. Mary of Egypt was asked, by the Abbot St. Zozimus, how she had been able to live forty-seven years in the desert where he found her dying. She answered : ' *With the hope of Paradise*'. If we be animated with the same hope, we shall not feel the tribulations of this life. Have courage ! Let us love God and labour for heaven. There the saints expect us, Mary expects us, Jesus Christ expects us. He holds in His hand a crown *to make each of us a king in that eternal kingdom* " (*Sermon* xvi.).

143. " Then shall the eyes of the blind be opened, and the ears of the deaf shall be unstopped. Then shall the lame man leap as a hart, and the tongue of the dumb shall be free. The land shall bud forth and blossom ; the glory of Libánus is given to it, the beauty of Carmel and Saron ; they shall see the glory of the Lord and the beauty of our God.

"Strengthen ye the feeble hands, and confirm the weak knees. Say to the faint-hearted, Take courage, fear not; behold your God will bring *the revenge of recompense.*

"And a path and a way shall be there; and it shall be called the holy way. The unclean shall not pass over it, nor fools err therein. No lion shall be there, nor shall any mischievous beast go up by it, nor be found there; *but they shall walk there that shall be delivered:* And the redeemed of the Lord shall return, and shall come with praise; and everlasting joy shall be upon their heads; they shall obtain joy and gladness; and sorrow and mourning shall fly away" (*Isaias* xxxv.).

THE END.

Made in the USA
Monee, IL
14 July 2024

61785393R00154